Published by **RELIANCE BOOKS COMPANY, LLC**

www.RelianceBooks.com

Email: Contact@RelianceBooks.com

ORDERING INFORMATION - **Quantity Sales:** Special discounts are available on quantity purchases by educational institutions and some other qualifying groups. For details, contact the 'Special Sales' department or see our website.

Individual Sales: Reliance books publications are available at many bookstores as well as on Amazon.com. They can also be ordered directly from Reliance Books.

Printed in The United States of America.

Knerr, Kreigh A.
Tips from the Top: A Tutor to the 1% Reveals His Tricks / Kreigh A. Knerr

p. cm.

ISBN-13: 978-0970990-88-4 (paperback)
ISBN-13: 978-0970990-89-1 (electronic)

1. Test Prep. 2. SAT Prep. 3. ACT Prep. 4. SAT Tutoring
5. ACT Tutoring.

"SAT" is a registered trademark of the College Board, which has no affiliation with and does not endorse this book. "PSAT/NMSQT" is a registered trademark of the College Board and the National Merit Scholarship Corporation, which also has no affiliation with and does not endorse this book. "ACT" is a registered trademark of ACT, Inc., which has no affiliation with and does not endorse this book (thank God).

Tips from the Top:

A Tutor to the 1% Reveals His Tricks

Kreigh A. Knerr

To Erin, the first student to tell me that I should write a book, any book, and she would read it. Thanks for inspiring me.

Table of Contents

Introduction: Why I Wrote This Book

People sometimes ask me, "What makes you an expert?" I find the question interesting because of the variety of tones in which it's asked, tones ranging from hostile antagonism to wide-eyed curiosity.

In test prep, expertise can mean all manner of things. It can mean you got hired by some larger company and they gave you a book that its team of "experts" wrote that you now have to implement. It can mean you have a teaching credential, which means you somehow are an expert in standardized testing too. It can mean you understand psychometrics. "Test prep expert" can mean all manner of things, which is why there are so many test prep experts running around today.

I've heard arguments that the test prep industry should be regulated, and I simply have to laugh. Many of the worst companies out there would easily meet regulations. I remember a student a few years ago who, after having worked with a national tutoring chain, asked me in her very first session whether I knew what the difference was between a semicolon and colon. Because we were covering reading and I hadn't assigned any homework on semicolons or colons, I asked her why this question had just sprung into her mind. "Well," she said, "when I was working with [the national tutoring chain], the tutors there didn't know the difference." Those tutors, by the way, were certified teachers, too. Somehow, I don't think regulation will resolve the vast disparities in skill from one test prep company to another.

Establishing expertise, then, isn't the easiest of tasks for families. How do you tell if a tutor is any good if there's such disparity? Typically, the measure of a tutor's quality comes from the recommendations of other families who have worked with that tutor. That's how almost all of my students find me. I'll often get phone calls that begin with a litany of former student and parent names and end with pleas to take on this new student who is a friend of theirs.

Of course, not everyone is so forthcoming about sharing their tutors. I have been "He Who Shall Not Be Named" at some prep schools because the students who attend them are so competitive that they won't even share the name of their SAT or ACT tutor with their classmates. Not all of the students at these high schools are that crazy-competitive, but when they try to bring up their shared tutoring experience with one of their more competitive classmates, they are quickly shushed and told, "We can't discuss him here."

While I think many people might find the Voldemort parallel only too apropos for someone who works in test prep, I find the secrecy surrounding myself and other 1% tutors the more interesting part of that story. (Yes, there are many tutors to the 1%. Look at the US population and do the math. One tutor couldn't possibly account for every 1% family.) I've been struck over the years by the number of articles about "how the other half lives" and the general sense that there's information out there that the rest of us don't have access to. The test prep industry as a whole feasts on such fears, I'm well aware. I am not, however, a mass-market corporation in the test prep industry with an ever-expanding appetite. As an individual, I don't have to play by the rules of the game that others do.

(Because it's such a titillating idea that some people can't let go of, I will tell you the secret sauce that 1% clients have that the rest of us don't: time. Mental time, physical time, time. Next to using excellent resources and having tutors or teachers who are at least borderline competent [something folks in the 1% can even struggle to find], the mental time or space most students require to improve their scores is hard to come by.)

The purpose of this book is to reveal the resources, the research, and the rolling conversations that my students benefit from and deeply value. I've written it because I find it disgusting when people in my industry parade around their 1% clients as if those in the 1% were the only ones who could get access to world-class test prep, which isn't true. I've written it because teachers so frequently ask me how they're supposed to handle the ridiculousness of the ACT and SAT.

I've written it for the schools, teachers, and volunteer tutoring centers I train. I've written it because the SAT and ACT in particular are severely flawed tests that deserve broad censure. I've written it for the hundreds of students I can't work with because my schedule is already full. I've written it because my students wanted me to.

This book isn't a step-by-step manual with a ten-week preparation plan, though I have a chapter that does just that. Those books already exist. This book isn't a mere listing of "tips and tricks" in the common sense. This book is the product of the thousands of students with whom I've worked. Its insights are those that are, for the most part, distinct to me and my research. Students often tell me that they learned more in their first session with me than in all the test prep they did prior. That first session is accounted for almost word-for-word in the next three chapters.

Feel free to read this book through from beginning to end. It's intended to be engaged in that manner. You may also read individual chapters as they pique your interest. This book works just as well that way, though any two-part chapters should be read in order. If you want to know why I'm an expert, I believe this book will answer that question for you.

Now let's do this. It's time to improve your understanding of the ACT and SAT and boost those scores.

Chapter 1: Read

Read. Just read. The solution is simple, yet it's also vague. What should I read? When should I read? Why should I read?

It's the last question that carries the most weight. Plenty of people say "I hate reading." In fact, I say that some days, though I typically complain more about writing because I have to work much harder at it. But it's the rare bird who truly hates *all* reading. Typically, we all hate some reading. We also tend to embrace other types of reading. Our mission: to find those types you like and build from there.

I still haven't answered the question, though, have I? You should read so that you don't have to accept the universal authority of Google, *The New York Times*, or College Board. You should read so that you can experience a life other than your own. You should read so that you can compellingly narrate your own experiences. You should read so that you can live the life you dream.

It's that last sentence that matters. Living the dream takes work, certainly. But those ephemeral moments when your dreams drift right along with your real life make the work worthwhile. So let's look at the things that you should read. And then let's think about that when-you-should-read business.

I should make a small comment, though, before we begin. I'll let Arthur L. Humphreys unpack it, because you'll probably get a lot of advice from every third uncle and cousin twice removed as you're applying to college:

"Be very careful about reading books which are recommended, because they are books of the hour. Fools step in and say read this and that without thinking to put themselves in your place. Because a book suits one person, it is only a rare chance that it will suit a friend equally."

My goal is to put myself in your shoes as best I can from within a book's pages. If you have specific questions about a genre, feel free to ask me on Twitter (@QuotEdapp). I'll do my best to answer there or in a blog post on my website. I've helped thousands of students test better, and I spend most of my time investigating ways to improve the success of my students on their tests and in life. Or to put it another way, if it truly does take 10,000 hours to reach mastery in something, I've more than tripled that total and I don't intend to stop my autodidactic investigations.

So let's launch into five books that I know can make your SAT and ACT adventures more enjoyable and more successful:

1) *Outliers* by Malcolm Gladwell

Since you're reading *Tips from the Top,* you probably don't have a tutor for your SAT and ACT prep. So you need some inspiration. Yes, you'll need encouragement along the way, but this book is the kickstarter to your testing campaign.

Not only is *Outliers* really easy to read, but it'll also introduce you to a bevy of characters who achieved success through uncommon means. Further, you'll be reading about people like you. How do I know that? Only an outlier would have picked up this book. Let *Outliers* inspire you to even greater success.

Oh, and as an added bonus, Malcolm Gladwell's writing has actually been used by the ACT for its passages before, so you'll be strengthening your ACT and SAT reading skills in the least painful way possible. Win win.

When should you read it? The second you finish reading *Tips from the Top.* Order it online, go to a bookstore, or go to the library and grab it immediately.

2) *They Say, I Say,* 3rd edition without readings by Gerald Graff and Cathy Birkenstein

Have you ever complained that what you study in school is useless once you get out? Well, you won't be able to make that argument this time. In fact, I've used the strategies advocated in *They Say, I Say* to enhance my own business. My marketing has improved, and I've been featured on CNN, Inc., Huff Post, and many other outlets just by implementing the strategies in *They Say, I Say*.

Now that we've got the "well, here's another useless book" card off the table, let's see what *They Say, I Say* has to offer specifically for your SAT and ACT studies.

First, *They Say, I Say* will introduce you to the world of academic writing. Not in a boring, please-make-it-stop way, but with penetrating insights into how academic writing gets structured. In case you're wondering why this matters, that's precisely the sort of writing you'll see on the ACT or SAT. Once you're introduced to academic writing's tricks, you should have a pretty decent chance of handling them when they show up on the SAT and ACT. And they will show up.

Second, *They Say, I Say* will help strengthen your knowledge of transitional words and phrases. For example, you'll learn when to use "although" and when to use "because"—this sentence even began with a transition, "For example." While comprehending transitions might not seem like a big deal, I can't tell you how frequently students mess these up on the ACT and in their own writing. Plus, transitions are a critical element in academic writing, which, again, is what you will be seeing on the ACT and SAT (and, shockingly enough, in college!).

Although many of the exercises at the end of each chapter can be ignored if you don't have that much practice time, Exercise 1 in Chapter 8 absolutely needs to be done because it shows you the inner workings of transitions. Ask an English teacher to review your work once you've completed it. But I don't just want you to do Ex. 1 in Chapter 8. I want you to read Chapter 8 without doing Ex. 1. After you've finished reading *They Say, I Say* all the way through, you should go back to reread Chapter 8 and then do Ex. 1. You'll have to take my word on this, but then again, you are already reading this book, so I'm guessing you didn't pick it up to question every suggestion made in it.

Third, *They Say, I Say* will improve your ability to read science papers and studies. This ability is exactly what the ACT Science section and Natural Science subsection of ACT Reading purport to evaluate and what the SAT has now decided to include in its reading section. I'll be honest, I don't think anyone ever taught me how to read scientific journals. That skill was just expected or assumed. Eventually, I learned to hack my way through such journals, but I imagine you're like me and would prefer if it weren't quite so hard to reach that level of comfort. And even if you're not like me, I'm sure you'd like higher scores.

When should you read it? I like to have students read *They Say, I Say* starting ten to fifteen weeks before their test, just so that they can read one-two chapters per week. Since my students have crazy schedules, I often have to modify my preference. Basically, if you have at least five weeks before your next test, you'll have enough time to study. The best time to study *They Say, I Say*, though, is when you're actually in school. That way, even if unconsciously, you can practice what you're learning.

3) *The Art of Deception* by Nicholas Capaldi and Miles Smit

I have to admit that I had about three different books in contention for this spot. Since my primary concern is for you, my high school-aged readers, that made my decision a little bit easier. I know you'll love *Outliers*, and I believe you'll finish *They Say, I Say* ready to tackle your high school and college writing with much less pain than before. I also realize that those are two full books and that I'm going to be recommending two more still after this one. So I picked the best self-study manual for high school students to address a subject that is of the greatest importance for standardized test success: logic. We'll address this subject more in the next chapter, but *The Art of Deception* will be your back-pocket buddy when you're ready to build on that chapter.

At its heart, *The Art of Deception* sets out to teach you logic, both formal and informal. But instead of asking you to memorize all the Latin variations of deductively valid syllogisms (seriously, this is actually a thing), *The Art of Deception* explores how you can craftily win others to your viewpoint with every logical fallacy in the book. This approach engages you in such a friendly and amusing fashion that you'll find it easy to remember the reasoning structures that underpin everyday society *and* standardized tests. That's right, even as you go on a farcical journey into the land of logical subterfuge, you'll be building the precise skills you need to master the makers of the SAT and ACT.

When should you read it? This book is awesome, but it does require a modicum of mental work. My suggestion is to tackle it over a summer or winter break (or a two-week spring break, if you're so lucky). If you don't have a break before your next test, and you really want to squeeze this book in before that test, then I'd suggest carving out seven Saturdays or Sundays so you can do one chapter each weekend.

4) *The Elements of Style* by William Strunk and E. B. White

Not gonna lie, this book elicits strong opinions. Some people love it; others despise it. Since I'm a pragmatist, I don't really care about strong opinions. What I do care about is that the first thirty-eight pages cover the bulk of what you'll need for SAT and ACT grammar. The fifth chapter is a pretty nice aid as well, but if you just forced yourself to comprehend every inch of those opening thirty-eight pages, you'd find yourself a master of "standard written English."
Now here's why I use this book with all my students: grammar is

guided by both your ear and your intellect. Sometimes your ear will be able to catch an inapt phrase because it just sounds "off." Other times, though, your ear will actually mislead you, and you will need your intellect to help you recover so that your writing avoids appearing nonsensical. The S&W (that's how I abbreviate Strunk and White when I'm assigning sections of their book to my students) not only strengthens your grammatical intellect, but it also strengthens your grammatical ear.

I'll be honest, I researched over thirty grammar books trying to make certain that I was using the best one with my students. Thirty! Do you have any idea how mind-numbingly awful that is? My favorite part in some of those books was when they'd complain about *The Elements of Style* and then proceed to exacerbate every supposed error that William Strunk and E. B. White had unwittingly thrust upon their readers. One even complained that you can't understand some of the words in *The Elements of Style* (this is true of maybe five words, but that's what Google and teachers are for) and then propped up his prose with words that I didn't even know existed. If you're going to complain about something, please don't make it worse! All of that to say, there are other grammar books in existence. Use them at your own peril. My students and I will take the thirty-eight pages of S&W pain over thirty books that will be less helpful.

I'll come back to S&W in Chapter 11 where I map out a ten-week course of study you can use for both SAT and ACT.

When should you read it? One subsection per day, on repeat until you're living and breathing the suggestions made in those thirty-eight pages. The English section generally makes for the easiest section to improve on either the SAT or the ACT. Find a used copy of S&W for a buck and have at it bit by bit.

5) *Microstyle* by Christopher Johnson

What's that you say, you've never heard of it? Of course. I had to throw in one curveball. And a book with an invented word for its title seemed an inspired pitch.

While the micro-message has always been in vogue (e.g. "Know Thyself"), our present culture's move back towards the freelance entrepreneur and replacement of the town crier with Twitter require us to enter the world of micro-messaging. Whether it's your resume, your application essay, or your ACT and SAT essays, a mastery of microstyle will allow your arguments to shine.

You see, the first two books I've listed will assist you as you learn big-picture writing. The second two books will improve your internal logic as you move from the idea of a whole essay or whole blog post down to an individual paragraph or sentence. *Microstyle* will take those individual sentences and help you to consider how they work independently and how they work in unison. Simply put, *Microstyle* will teach you to make your sentences pop.

When should you read it? Once you've finished the books listed above, dive in!

Yes, shockingly enough, there *is* a method to my madness, and that method will make you a better dreamer and a better test-taker. As you learn to tell stories in a thousand words and in five words, and as you learn to construct brief arguments and well-developed arguments, you'll find yourself prepared for any challenges you face in school, on tests, and in that mythical reality called "the real world."

So read. Read anything. Read broadly and read deeply. And if you don't have time to read anything else, read the five books listed above. Then let me know which you liked best!

"The reason why so many people who read much know so little, is because they read isolated books instead of reading one book in connexion with another. The memory is trained by association, and if you read two books in succession on one subject you know more than twice as much as if you had read one book only." Arthur L. Humphreys

"Students sometimes acquire the habit of reading single sentences at a time, then of writing them down, thinking that by making an exact copy of the book, they are playing safe. This is a pernicious practice; it spoils continuity of thought and application. Furthermore, isolated sentences mean little, and fail grossly to represent the real thought of the author. A better way is to read through an entire paragraph or section, then close the book and reproduce in your own words what you have read." Harry D. Kitson

Chapter 2: Reason, Part the First

These next two chapters are gonna roll in dialogue format in places. Why? Well, it's mostly because I can't write them any other way. I always teach standardized test reasoning as part of a conversation with my students at their very first session. I'm only able to win their confidence in my research-based approach to standardized test reasoning by letting them ask me their most pressing questions about it. So we'll approach these two chapters using the exact model I use with my one-on-one students. If I haven't managed to address your questions by the end of this and the next chapter, email me. The purpose of this book is that you benefit from the training contained within its pages. If you're uncertain about something I've written, that's a great time to ask a question. I've done my best to anticipate any questions, but I know people always have more.

I should note that these chapters will address reasoning that is to be employed *after* you've read a passage, not prior to reading a passage. This includes Reading, Science, and English/Writing and Language passages.

My first point will be perhaps the simplest and because of that the most offensive to your sophisticated brilliance. Nevertheless, it will be of import. Ready? Before you start navigating any question that involves reading within the question (this basically includes every single ACT or SAT question that isn't about English punctuation or phrasing), *cover up the answer choices* so your eyes don't see them.

This might seem strange. Why on earth would you cover up answer choices when analyzing and answering them is precisely what you need to do in order to get a semi-decent score? Well, it's because the ACT and SAT are a little sneaky about something. You see, when they tell you you're taking a reading comprehension test, what they don't tell you is that the questions on that test are as much of the reading comprehension test as the passages themselves. Most people focus on the passage and on the answer choices, but they leap right over the questions. You know, because the answer choices are where you get to fill in the bubbles, finish the test, and go home to take a nap.

I get it. I really do. I have to force myself to cover up the answer choices. Otherwise, my eyes blitz past the question into the answer choices or keep flicking down to answer choices while I'm still ~~reading~~ scanning the question. By covering up the answer choices, you force your eyes to fixate on the only thing that should be important at that moment. Here's the thing: good readers in particular are notorious for reading past the question to get into the answer choices. Why? Because good readers often take in a paragraph as a whole, if you will. They don't over-read by focusing on each individual word. With the questions, though, focusing on each individual word becomes essential, or at least noting the key words does.

Before we get into key words, I must mention a story from two years ago. I had not one, but two!, students who decided to tell me after their preparations with me that the most helpful thing that I taught them was covering up the answers.[1] After at first wondering what I was doing with my life—if this was indeed the most helpful thing I'd taught someone—I decided to get over myself and acknowledge what they meant: for them, skimming by the question had cost them two or three questions a section. For most people, it's really only worth about one question a section. You decide how much you like missing a question. I personally don't. Missing a question usually means I've lost a point. I hate losing points, particularly when I miss them because of something I can easily correct. Yes, you'll look a little odd covering up answer choices, but who will be watching you when they're taking the test themselves?!

All righty, let's get back to what we're supposed to *find* in those questions. I used to be able to joke about my job whenever people

---

[1] Your obvious takeaway is that you can just ignore the rest of this book. I've covered all the essentials now…

asked me what I did for a living. I said that I taught people to read the word "not." It was a great joke,[2] and then the stupid SAT had to get updated and remove the NOT questions.[3] Talk about killing someone's game.

For the ACT, though, qualifiers like "NOT" and "EXCEPT" can be found right alongside other standardized testing fan favorites like "first," "only," and "last." For both the ACT and SAT, qualifiers will be intermingled with and often replaced by what I like to call descriptive labels. The question may ask you, for example, about a purple hot air balloon. Well, if you get super excited about the word "balloon," you may find yourself back in the passage where it talks about a *yellow* hot air balloon. But it's guaranteed that the yellow hot air balloon is going to have different properties from the purple hot air balloon. Agh! Now descriptive labels may be a touch more difficult than offering a simple color test[4]—they may instead ask you to find the three-legged stool (as

---

[2] It also prevented people from telling me about their horrible experiences while taking standardized tests, how standardized tests ruined their lives, and how some people are just bad test-takers. First things first, if you'd like to hear *my thoughts* on bad test-takers, please check out chapter 8. Second, I'm not your flipping therapist! I'm not getting paid to hear about your life's struggles. Unless you're presently one of my high school students, I legitimately don't care. You're twenty-eight for Pete's sake. Get over it! Do you have a paying job? Yes? And you're still talking about standardized tests? Do you have any hobbies, other life experiences? …No? Well, my new acquaintance, you're what we like to call a life buzzkill. You're sucking the life from the rest of us. (I do actually care about how my own students experience the test. You're in high school. The standardized tests are sucking the life out of you. That's a legit complaint, and I do need to know how you're experiencing the test so I can help you improve. But once you're out of college and done with standardized tests, I don't want to hear about how you struggled on standardized tests. The struggle isn't real anymore. It's back in your adolescence. Please leave it there along with your high school fashion choices.)

[3] Well, they still appear in math questions, but they don't overrun the reading and English sections anymore.

[4] Though I can't tell you how many students miss simple color questions on the English and Science tests. Seriously kids, know your colors. They were covered in kindergarten. Don't miss these questions. It's embarrassing. Also, I'm not referencing Dr. Max Lüscher's infamous color test. That's a fun test and all, but not applicable here (or perhaps anywhere, but I'll leave that to the psychologists and philosophers of mind to debate).

opposed to the four-legged stool). You might think I'm joking about the simplicity of these descriptive labels. I'm not.

Sidebar: this is a point that I'll probably mention again, but please remember that the ACT and SAT *can't always be tricky*. Yes, they have to create a number of nasty questions so that they can swiftly sift adept learners into somewhat arbitrary, statistical categories. But not everyone is scoring a 36 or 800. That means that there need to be a few questions that *are* easy. Don't let simplicity make your head swim.

Back to descriptive labels: I once had a student ask me if the ACT was simply a glorified synonym search. I responded that I've often noted that people who were word-search aficionados back in the day tend to be awesome "readers" on the ACT. In fact, I had a different student who was so bad at the ACT's word-search game (on occasion, a synonym search when the ACT wants to get tricky) that I assigned him daily word searches. It helped. I'd never done it before; I hope to never do it again, but I will if another student finds that the ACT's super duper fun game of find-the-missing-word isn't so fun.[5]

All right, enterprising student (ES). The promised dialogue is upon you. It'll appear at the start to be merely a hefty monologue, but I promise your questions will be accounted for!

Kreigh: After you've read the question—and fully comprehended

---

[5] Footnotes are great, right? This is actually a psychology experiment to see which of you dare to plumb the depths of my footnotes. If you're wondering how that experiment could be conducted in a printed book, you've probably also realized that I'm not actually conducting an experiment. Footnotes are where I add sidebar comments to distract you from actually learning, kind of like ACT and SAT prep do. ACT fun fact: the reading comprehension the ACT is so focused upon—rapidly scanning a passage to find a hidden word—is the same reading comprehension that has been displaced in legal offices by algorithmic word searches. That's right, one of the major 21st century "college and career readiness" skills the ACT places an emphasis on evaluating is already an automated skill that humans are no longer needed for in law firms. You do you, ACT. We feel so much more ready for our careers now. Think that algorithm might need a personal assistant? …study buddy? …no?

it—I'd like you to come up with your own answer. I don't care whether you remember some specific thing you read or you quickly glance back at the text to find information that relates to the question. Most people do a hybrid of those two things. Sometimes they remember what they've read; sometimes they recall it appearing somewhere near the third paragraph so they go back to look there.

Most tutors will agree with the idea of coming up with your own answer. "Think of an answer before you dive into the answer choices" is a pretty standard piece of standardized testing advice. The problem that I run into with other folks in test prep is when they *add* to that proposition. You see, they aren't content to just tell people to think of an answer they want to find. They are compelled for some reason to expand their proposition to include "and then go find it."

This expansion of the proposition is where those other tutors and I must part ways. This parting is for two reasons. First, have you ever thought of an answer choice and then looked through the answer choices only to find that it wasn't there?

ES: Ugh, yeah.

Kreigh: It's like "what the crap?"

ES: It's literally the worst. I just want to drop my pencil and leave.[6]

Kreigh: That's about your only option. I mean seriously. You're told to think of an answer and then go find it, but when it isn't there, what do you do?!

ES: Yeah… pretty much nothing. Ugh.

---

[6] I should note that this conversation has many variations at this point. Sometimes I say that it's literally the worst. Sometimes students insert more colorful language to express their emotions in such a moment. Overall, this conversation is representative enough of the one we'd probably have at this point.

Kreigh: So that's reason number one. If your answer isn't there, you're pretty much screwed because your plan of attack resulted in a whole lot of nothing. If I don't just give up, I'm gonna let out a primal roar of frustration, which probably doesn't do anything to help me out.

ES: (unhappy look slowly spreading across face)

Kreigh: But the second reason is even more important. Remember, the ACT and SAT have to make it so that you miss questions; otherwise they can't produce their pretty little population segments.[7] There are two primary considerations that you can have about people missing questions. Either reasonably intelligent people are missing questions *or* only people who score 36s and 800s are reasonably intelligent. I prefer the former option. I've coached perfect idiots to perfect scores whom I'd never trust as my doctor or in just about any other role, and I've met many perfectly bright people who didn't score perfectly on a standardized test.[8]

Given my experience, I prefer to believe that the standardized test questions are intended to make reasonably intelligent people miss questions. Since I'm your tutor, you're kind of stuck with me believing that, but I don't expect you to believe it. If we were to

---

[7] You, sir, are a 95th percentile. And you, miss, are a 99th percentile. Do you feel special, unspecial, or android-like?

[8] This is not, however, to allow for the immediate insertion of trivial formulas such as "I may not be book smart, but at least I'm street smart." First, there isn't a universal dichotomy between book smarts and street smarts—a person can possess both. People often make the dichotomy simply so that they don't have to acquire both. Intellectual laziness is just a different sort of intellectual snobbery. Second, and this is perhaps more interesting, *what street are you on*? There are quite a few streets where I feel at home. There are other streets where I simply haven't acquired the necessary experience or insights to thrive (or even survive). Perhaps they can be learned for each context (indeed, on streets in non-English speaking countries, I'd need to learn the language, too.). I acknowledge that both book smarts and streets smarts are kinds of intelligence, but their existence doesn't produce an unresolvable dilemma that prevents the acquisition of both kinds. That is, they aren't mutually exclusive.

continue with my assumptions about the world a bit further, though, we'd then have to ask ourselves, how *do* you make reasonably intelligent people miss questions?

ES: BS[9]?

Kreigh: I typically go with "shenanigans," but yes. And do you know the easiest way of creating the shenanigans which will make reasonably intelligent people miss questions?

ES: (mostly wondering what shenanigans *I'm* up to)

Kreigh: You take the answer that comes most readily to mind for the majority of people and you do something terrible to it.

ES: . . .

Kreigh: You see, test-writers tend to be lazy, and the easiest way to confuse people is to take that answer choice that comes most readily to mind for the majority of people and do terrible things to it. Of course, this is where the "and then go find it!" portion of the proposition becomes distinctly problematic. Because if we're hunting for that answer choice that we've thought of, we now have blinders on. Only our answer choice will satisfy our insatiable desire for scantron dominance. Unfortunately, our blinders[10] will not help us to identify the shenanigans the ACT and SAT[11] have in store for us because our blinders have led us to the very answer choice we should be most worried about.

---

[9] It's probably 50-50 whether students call BS or just give me a quizzical (and worried) look.

[10] You could also refer to this as "tunnel vision."

[11] PSA: if the SAT is now using "small words" or "everyday language" in its questions and answer choices, it still has to generate its statistical segments somehow. Believe it or not, you can confuse people by using everyday language. Believe the SAT's PR spin at your own peril. I'll pass on assuming the SAT intends to play nice.

In function, our answer choice will now morph into some sort of a beating stick or bludgeoning tool: ALL ANSWERS MUST SUBMIT TO ME! So if a given answer choice is only ninety percent of what our thought-up answer was, literally missing the two or three essential words that make the whole thing tick, then we try to use our beating stick to flatten that ninety percent answer into the shape of our thought-up answer's one hundred percent. If the answer includes some extra warts which negate what we wish to see, then we try to pulverize them to death with our bludgeoning tool. Here's the fun part: as much as it might *feel* like you're doing something, you aren't. I personally don't give a rip about how you feel; I care about how you score. You'll feel just fine after you have an improved score. Feeling like you've done something when you haven't is rather pointless and will not help your score. Your pencil's scratching out or adding of information doesn't actually do those things to a live ACT or SAT. You can't change the answers, so your weird-world beating stick is simply from a parallel universe. Please come back to this one.

Now at this point you might be wondering why on earth I've suggested that you come up with your own answer choice if it does all of these horrible things to you.

ES: (looking at me with a mixture of horror, confusion, and hope[12])

Kreigh: Well, it does all of these horrible things to you when you've decided that this is *the* answer and the only possible answer. When all answers must submit to the great and terrible answer you've come up with, then yeah, you're pretty much screwed. Way to play into the test-designer's hands.

However, when you put your answer off to the side and say this is what *a* possible good answer could look like, then you've given yourself a fighting chance. Now your answer is working as a

---

[12] Not hope that I'll offer something to resolve this apparent insanity, but rather hope that *I'll* get off the crazy train. Sorry kids, I'm tethered to it. At least be happy that you're reading this instead of working with me in person.

measuring stick against which you can evaluate all of the ACT and SAT's answer choices. No longer are you stuck saying "well, shoot…" when your answer isn't there.

Using your thought-up answer choice also helps to keep the reasoning process in the order that it should be. People tend to get bogged down when they decide on their answer choice and then elect to deliberate whether it's a good one. Funny story: effective reasoning typically works the other way. You deliberate *and then* you decide. This was known at least as far back as Aristotle's time. When people waffle (aka deliberate) *after* they've already decided, it makes no sense. It does, however, waste time and make it more likely that you'll talk yourself out of a good answer or into a bad one.

When you have *a* possible good answer in mind, you can delay your decision as long as possible, which is what we want. As Aristotle would say, "we deliberate a long time, but decide quickly." Use your answer as that measuring stick. Do the given answer choices measure up to it? The question isn't whether they match; the question is whether they are qualitatively worth considering. Deliberate. Then decide.

ES: Okay, yeah, that actually does make sense. (secretly hoping this is where the conversation ends…[13])

---

[13] But… just like an irrepressible salesperson at a county fair, I've got a "But wait, there's more!" coming your way.

"In the days of thy youth seek to obtain that which shall compensate the losses of thy old age. And if thou understandest that old age is fed with wisdom, so conduct thyself in the days of thy youth that sustenance may not be lacking to thy old age." Leonardo da Vinci

"He who in reasoning cites authority is making use of his memory rather than of his intellect." Leonardo da Vinci

"A good memory is a memory which assimilates. Every one has a good memory for something. A good memory rejects and sifts, and does not accept everything offered to it like a pillar-box." Arthur L. Humphreys

"Originality may perhaps be defined as the power of abstracting for oneself, and is in thought what strength of mind is in action. Our opinions are commonly derived from education and society. Common minds transmit as they receive, good and bad, true and false; minds of original talent feel a continual propensity to investigate subjects and strike out views for themselves;—so that even old and established truths do not escape modification and accidental change when subjected to this process of mental digestion." John Henry Newman

"To doubt everything or to believe everything are two equally convenient solutions; both dispense with the necessity of reflection." Henri Poincaré

Chapter 3: Reason, Part the Second

Before we get into this chapter, I want you to reference your official ACT or SAT prep book. If you don't have either of those prep books, do a quick internet search for "free official practice ACT PDF [SAT PDF]." You should find what you need. Now, go to one of the reading tests. I'll wait...

Find one? Let's get into this.

Kreigh: So what kind of an answer choice does the SAT or ACT ask you to find in the directions?

ES: Um...

Kreigh: I'm asking the Captain Obvious question, I promise. It really is that simple. What kind of an answer are you supposed to find?

ES: The best?

Kreigh: That's right, the best. Note that the directions don't say the right, the correct, the perfect, or the only. That's a very particular word choice.

ES: (varied responses, but generally it's a silent response of discomfort and uncertainty)

Kreigh: Those directions are partly there so the test-makers can't get sued.

ES: What the...?

Kreigh: I wish I were joking. But if they said "right answer," you'd be able to sue if you came up with an answer that worked but that they didn't like. You see, by choosing "best answer," the ACT and

SAT have constructed a specific control on the test that puts all sorts of possibilities in play. When you're playing the game of "best answer," that means *multiple* answers can be right. But there's only one best answer.

It also means that there could be no right answers. This typically only happens if the test-writers screw up on writing the ACT or SAT questions, but it can happen.[14]

Here's where things get a bit awkward, though. When you're in school, what sort of answer are you typically looking for?

ES: The right answer.

Kreigh: Precisely. But on the ACT and SAT, there is no such thing as a right answer.[15] There is only the *best answer*. Now, it is possible to say that when we say "right answer" we simply mean "best answer," and I won't entirely disagree with that colloquialism. But "right answer" has other colloquial meanings, including "true" or "only possible." These additional meanings get us into trouble when we're trying to think clearly about the reasoning structures of the ACT and SAT.

---

[14] We see you there, question 40 on page 157 of *The Real ACT Prep Guide, 3rd Ed.* Way to go ACT, you've managed to publish for all the world to see that you don't know how logic and language work together. A little hint, reasonable people could select F *or* H. There isn't a best answer between them. Perhaps if you'd made the important semantic switch from "would think" to "could think" in answer choice F, you'd have an argument for asking us readers to distinguish between F and H. But you didn't, dear ACT. Instead, you've revealed that you either don't understand language usage (awkward for a test that declares it tests just that) or that you expect people to reach your conclusion in some arbitrary fashion, which would be to ignore the reasonable person standard upon which American law and government rest. Reasonable people *would* find it impossible to reach agreement on an answer from amongst your choices on this question, ACT. But thank you for showing the world that even a team of "experts" can create a question that a reasonable person cannot answer. Yay?

[15] Well, on the ACT's Math section, you are asked to find the "correct answer." The SAT's Math sections still say "best answer." All other sections of both tests ask for the "best answer."

See, true/false reasoning (or right/wrong reasoning, as we typically think of it) means that an answer is true because it's true or false because it's false. It's like living in a perfect deductive reasoning world, one where answers exist *independently of each other*. But the SAT and ACT say that you are supposed to find the "best answer," not the right or true answer.

Sometimes this is where people look at me and think, "this fool is just fixating on a meaningless exercise in semantics." Perhaps. But you see, this is one of those rare moments in everyday life when a semantic difference presents a distinctively *meaningful difference*. If the test-makers say that we are to choose the best answer, that opens up a new realm of answer choices for them, which is to our severe disadvantage. It's now possible to have multiple right answers to a question: we simply must find the best one. In fact, it's even possible to have *no right answers* at all, which forces us to select the answer choice with the fewest flaws.

Asking for someone to find the best answer means that there has to be a relationship and a hierarchy amongst the answer choices. You literally cannot be the best at anything without at least two other options against which you can be compared.[16] In the case of the ACT and SAT, you have four options which you have to relate to each other and see which one rises to the top of the bunch.

Other tutors and test prep books drive me nuts when they tell students to find the right answers. Why? Because that's asking students to employ a reasoning structure that is ill-fitting to the test.[17]

---

[16] Remember elementary school: you are *good* at rollerblading; you are *better* than Romeo at rollerblading; when you go rollerblading with Romeo and Regina, you are the *best* at it.

[17] Or, if you wish to submit that "right answer" can mean both "only possible answer" and "best answer," then you're still stuck with the fact that—as an individual test-taker who is under a severe time constraint—you have to keep clear in your brain in the midst of the test that you are employing the "best answer" colloquial meaning of "right answer" instead of "only possible answer." Do you really want to be doing that intellectual dance all while you're trying to figure out

When the ACT and SAT say best answer in their directions, they mean best answer. This isn't to say that best answer is necessarily the nicest of rules to put on the test. "Best answer" can mean both "answer agreed upon by the majority of college-educated individuals" and "answer agreed upon by a team of education experts," which makes our task as test-takers a bit unfortunate.[18] But "best answer" does mean "best answer," not "true" or "only answer." That much we have to keep clear.

Basically, when people tell you to find the right answer, they aren't giving you an impossible task; they are giving you a much harder way of approaching things, one which may not work out so well at times.

ES: Okay, that kind of makes sense, but why does that affect how I go about the test?

Kreigh: Mostly because this meaningful difference also alters the form of reasoning by which we should approach the test. The way multiple choice test strategy is often taught, you'd be led to think that one answer is right and the rest are wrong, but that would be true/false or binary thinking. But best-answer reasoning—that is, the reasoning the tests *tell us we're supposed to use*—is not fundamentally rooted in a true/false paradigm.

Let's try an analogy to clarify the distinction. Have you ever put together a bookshelf?

ES: Oh yeah (or… No, not really)

Kreigh: Okay, well imagine you are putting together a bookshelf in

---

how the crap the ACT or SAT is trying to confuse you? Really?! Please remember that there are no hero points for making your task harder. Just stupid points awarded to you by you.

[18] "Best answer" could mean other things, too, but the two given here seem to be the meanings the ACT and SAT seek to hide behind in general. Isn't it great that the ACT and SAT have so much fun with semantics?

your college dorm room. You've got a few tools with you, among them a flat-head screwdriver. As you are about to use your screwdriver in your bookshelf's assembly, you notice that you have a Phillips-head ("crosshead") screw. I don't know if you've ever tried to use a flat-head screwdriver in place of a Phillips-head screwdriver when a Phillips-head screwdriver is called for, but I can tell you that it can be a difficult process to turn the screw without completely wearing out the head of the screw, a phenomenon commonly known as stripping the screw. Once a screw is stripped, it's nearly impossible to remove the screw should you ever need to (and there are occasions in which you would need to). Notice that it's possible to use a flat-head screw driver on a Phillips-head screw. The process, however, is usually awkward and can be potentially damaging to the screw or your furniture when you try to remove the screw.[19]

I'm guessing you're clever enough to figure out that the flat-head screwdriver is true/false reasoning and that the Phillips-head screw is the best-answer reasoning a standardized test question demands. Of course, no analogy is perfect, but I trust that this one gives you some idea that there is a meaningful distinction to be made between true/false reasoning and best-answer reasoning.

In true/false reasoning, all answer choices but one must necessarily be wrong, or false. That is, it is impossible for two answer choices to accurately answer a question. In best-answer reasoning, it is possible for two answers to be "true" or accurately answer a question, but one answer must exhibit traits that make it stronger than the other answer. Again, the other answer isn't wrong, but it is weaker, however slightly. I'm sure it sounds like I'm splitting hairs here, but the difference in true/false reasoning and best-answer reasoning is the difference between cognitive dissonance—unless you like looking at an answer that is "right" but somehow simultaneously "wrong"—and calm dismantling of the tests.

---

[19] I may or may not have personal experience with this. To quote one of many exquisite one-liners from the newer *The Italian Job*, "I had a bad experience."

To be bluntly binary myself, true/false reasoning is the wrong tool for a standardized test, unless you're being asked a question that involves a syllogism. That's the only exception I can think of.[20]

I should say, though, that some tutors (myself included) will acknowledge best-answer reasoning but then slip into "right and wrong" terminology just because it's so habitual. There is a difference, however, between using colloquial language *after* you've made clear that by "right and wrong" you're referring to "best answers and weaker answers" and using the colloquial "right and wrong" to reinforce a binary approach to the test. Personally, I strive to remove the "right and wrong" terminology from my speech, but even I slip up on occasion.

As a side note to those who've heard others declare that best-answer reasoning does not exist in the real world (I've heard this from teachers more than once), consider whether they really have thought through their claims. When you're choosing which college to attend, it's rare that you're choosing the "perfect school." Often, you're deciding which school has the most attributes you desire or which school has that one attribute you cannot live without. Neither of those scenarios presents a right answer. Your decision is simply the best one you can make given the information at hand. If you consider many of the decisions you make in everyday life, you will likely find that they are based on "imperfect," best-answer reasoning.[21]

You might be thinking about now that I've belabored the point about best-answer reasoning. Perhaps. But it's an essential thing to understand before we get to our next intellectual move to help us unlock the ACT and SAT (and really any standardized test that involves multiple choice). Ready for that?

---

[20] And those typically appear on the ACT's Math section. See footnote 2 in this chapter.

[21] For those of you who really like to geek out about this stuff, you're principally employing defeasible reasoning for the ACT and SAT with the occasional abductive reasoning appearance.

ES: I think I've got the gist of things.

Kreigh: I'm not a fan of the ACT and SAT's rules for finding the best answer. Why? Well, it's at least in part because our brains sometimes do a not-so-super-cool autocorrect of changing "best answer" to "right answer." It's wicked hard to get your brain fully into best-answer reasoning mode. And frankly, we already addressed the fact that the ACT and SAT only put the best-answer rules in play to make our lives harder. I don't like any of these things.

So instead of playing by the ACT and SAT's rules, I'm going to take their rules and flip them on their head. I'm going to hunt for the very worst possible answers they came up with. Curiously enough, this will automatically put me into a form of best-answering reasoning. If I'm steadily working my way through the worst answer choices, eventually I'll have to be left with the best.

ES: Why would I start working my way through all of the worst answer choices? Why not just hunt for the best answer and quickly get out of Dodge?

Kreigh: A most excellent question. Let's see if I can give you enough explanations that my proposal for navigating the questions seems reasonable. I simply ask that you let me get through all of my reasons and then ask follow-up questions as you see fit.

ES: Fair enough.

Kreigh: First, remember our previous discussion about how the ACT and SAT like to create their questions. They like to think of what comes most readily to mind for the majority of people and then screw with that very thing. The ACT and SAT's goal is to sort people into their pretty little categories, and they sort people by making them miss questions. I often suggest to students that they think of a test-writer as the crooked lawyer who's trying to rob them of their family inheritance. I once said this on NPR, and my host was quite worried about my statement. I had to restate that I had said the *crooked* lawyer, not just any random lawyer...

But once you have the idea in mind of people trying to screw you over, it makes sense to go hunting for how they're trying to screw you over. If a crooked lawyer were trying to take your money, you wouldn't just sit there and think to yourself "I wonder what delightful things this person hopes to accomplish with my inheritance." No, you'd sit there and say to yourself, "I know you're up to something, and I'm going to keep looking for it."

Students often start worrying at this point that looking for flaws is a bizarre sort of thing that no one would ever do and that they'll screw up their thinking if they go hunting for flaws. It's a fair worry.

...So tell me, do you have any siblings?

ES: Yes[22]

Kreigh: Older or younger?

ES: ...

Kreigh: Did they irritate you at all growing up? Just once or twice?

ES: (vigorous head nod)

Kreigh: Now this isn't confession time. I don't actually want to know about those occasions. But I'll bet if I asked you, you could probably list off a few things without even thinking about them. In fact, if I asked you to make a list of your sibling's flaws, you would likely produce that faster than a list of your sibling's good qualities.

---

[22] If no, I typically ask about cousins. If there are none of those, I skip down a bit in the conversation.

ES: (sheepish look)

Kreigh: But I don't say this to make you feel like a terrible sibling. I say this to note that as humans we are *awesome* fault finders. It mean, think about how you and your friends talk about your high school. How often do you find yourself dwelling on all of its wonderful attributes? Not often? …no? Perhaps you note some of its unfortunate quirks and the irritating individual personalities you encounter in its halls and classrooms instead. Yeah, I thought as much.

To look at it another way, whether you are working with a coach in sports or a teacher in the arts, what do they spend most of their time focusing on, the great things that everyone is doing or the flaws that need correcting? When you're editing your essays, what are you looking for? Weaknesses all around, right?

This, then, is the skill that we're trying to employ in the test: weakness hunting. It's totally natural to us as humans. We're just looking for flaws in an environment in which we hadn't thought to use that long-perfected skill.

Further, this allows us to reverse engineer the test. Remember, the easiest way to craft answer choices is to come up with a "best answer" and then do horrible things to it (i.e. add flaws to it). Well if we go hunting for the answers with flaws, we're essentially reverse engineering the test. We'll work our way back through the flawed answers to the best answer. I love reverse engineering the test because then the ACT and SAT don't get to control me. I'm using the test-makers' weapons against them.

People often ask me why I don't play video games anymore. I tell them I don't need to. I get to play with a real, live version of one, but one in which the outcome actually matters to my teammates in the game. Just as you have to navigate the closed-world assumptions of a video game, you have to navigate a similar set of closed-world assumptions on the ACT and SAT. And just like I used to spend hours in junior high figuring out how to create the fastest super team[23] in *Madden NFL*, I now spend innumerable hours making certain that the ACT and SAT's closed-world assumptions work against them.

ES: Okay, so I get the reverse engineering part and all the best-answer reasoning stuff, but won't I lose time? I mean, when I'm taking the test, my biggest struggle tends to be time.[24] Looking around for bad answers seems like it would waste a lot of time.

Kreigh: A fair query. There are two answers I can give you. First, my fundamental assumption as a tutor is that efficiency is the most important thing. What I mean by that is that I'm most concerned with how many questions you are able to answer *with the best answers* out of however many questions you see. For example, we could easily make it so that you see all forty questions on the ACT reading section, but if you only answer half of the questions with the best answers, you're going to walk out of there with approximately a 20 or 21 reading score. If, however, we were able to improve your efficiency to the point that you were able to get 90% of the questions per each reading subsection, and you only completed three of the four subsections, you'd still have twenty-seven of the forty questions in the bank, which would give you approximately a 24 or a 25 reading score. That doesn't include the additional two or three questions you could get from guessing on the last passage, which would push your score even higher.

Now of course my goal is that you're both seeing every passage and acing every passage, but my first priority is efficiency. Any nitwit can make it so that you're seeing every question. It's much harder work to improve how many best answers you're able to select. *That's* our job.

---

[23] Both fastest in terms of building an invincible team and in terms of outright footspeed for my players. I think I spent more time trading and picking up players on the waiver wire than I actually did playing the games. I was obsessed with winning and having the best team ever. I may have had a problem.

[24] There are a few students for whom speed is not the biggest problem. Fortunately for them, they need to focus on their technique (i.e. hunting for flaws).

Second answer to the speed problem. Have you ever noticed that Starbucks® basically advertises three sizes? While the Tall, Grande, and Venti® are the three people typically think of, you can also order a Short or a Trenta®. But why doesn't Starbucks constantly remind you of those two additional choices? Well, it's in part because Starbucks would jolly well like you to move the line along. The more options that people have, the more likely it is that they will get overwhelmed. The superabundance of choices leads to decision paralysis—people literally can't make a decision because they have too many options.[25] When I order at Starbucks, I'm ordering one of three sizes. And done.

But one of my local coffee shops, Colectivo, has decided to branch out with its sizing. You see, a small at Colectivo is 8oz. instead of the industry standard 12oz. Invariably, a drink order at Colectivo will take longer because when people order a small, the barista has to show them the tiny 8oz. cup and say, "This is a small. Are you sure?" and then the poor people have to hem and haw as they try to figure out whether they want a small, a 12oz. cup, or some other size. I now preempt the baristas at Colectivo when I order my 8oz. hot chocolate by telling them that "Yes, that really is the size I want." Who needs more than 8oz. of hot chocolate? Not me, anyway.

There's another local coffee shop that thinks it's neat to have an Italian-style macchiato instead of the HGH-enhanced version Starbucks puts out. But then the coffee shop baristas always have to ask me when I order a macchiato if I want a traditional macchiato, a larger, non-traditional macchiato, or a designer, HGH version. What I want is the macchiato that is advertised. Instead of a nice little caffeine hit early in the morning when I want to start writing, I now have to puzzle out what sort of drink I'd actually like. (A caffeinated one. That's the kind.) Fortunately, I've figured out to quickly include "Yes, the one on the board. The one you've advertised. Not the secret menu or gargantuan-sized editions."

---

[25] A related study showing that people can waste mental energy on little decisions when they have too many options has led to the visually stimulating wardrobes of entrepreneurs like Mark Zuckerberg.

Aside from revealing that I spend altogether too much time in coffee shops,[26] notice that when I'm ordering at these local coffee shops I have to know exactly what size I want before I order if I want to order swiftly. As my and other customers' options increase, we start to slow down the ordering line because we're trying to choose among the many options, even if we wanted a specific drink originally. It's the same thing on the ACT and SAT. When you're trying to process four answers at the same time, your brain literally can't process the information quickly. But when you're down to three answers or two, your brain is able to start reasoning faster.

We're trying to reduce the complexity for your brain. Further, if you keep rereading terrible answer choices—the ones you know are terrible at first glance—then you're wasting time on them. But if you physically cross them out, your brain won't have to think about them anymore.

Frankly, you might lose a second on a super easy question just because you'll have to process all of the answer choices. Then again, how will you know you've selected the best answer if you haven't seen all of them? And a better question, how do you know a question is easy until after you've answered it?

While you'll lose that second on a super easy question, looking for flaws will save you multiple seconds (sometimes minutes) on questions that range in difficulty from medium to crazy hard. Because you'll have used the super easy questions to get you in rhythm, though, you'll have a fighting chance on those nastier questions. And while you might only get a crazy hard question down to three options from the four given, that's still one fewer option that you have to think about! I'll take it.

So yes, you'll lose a fraction of time on those so-called super easy questions, but you'll gain that time back and then some on all the rest of the questions. And, you'll be in rhythm for those hard questions because you'll have used the easier ones as a warmup.

---

[26] I wonder if that has any correlation to my writing this book? No, couldn't be.

ES: Okay, that mostly makes sense.[27]

Kreigh: Awesome, because if you're still unsure, I do have the forty-hour version of this.

ES: Um, no thank you (but also looking at me half-thinking I must be kidding).

Kreigh: You know, I've surprisingly never had any takers for my forty-hour version, but if you look at my bookshelf in the other room, literally half of that second shelf is all about argumentation theory, defeasible reasoning, abductive reasoning, and other fun forms of informal logic. Those books account for maybe a quarter of my research into the delightful arena of the philosophical bedrock upon which standardized testing is built. Best-answer reasoning is baby play compared to that bookshelf. Are you sure you don't want the forty-hour version?

ES: No, just no. Can we get on with the ACT [SAT]?

Kreigh: Oh, I think I can handle that.

With that dialogue aside, I'm going to let Douglas Walton take it apart with a little insight that may resonate with those of you who have taken a timed standardized test before,[28] mostly because he's pretty much the boss when it comes to practical reasoning:[29]

---

[27] I think a healthy 95% of my students truly give me intellectual assent here. Unfortunately, only about eighty percent of that ninety-five percent follow through with that intellectual assent on their first week of homework. It takes at least two weeks for the remaining twenty percent of that ninety-five percent to actually implement technique. Yeah, it's a rough few weeks for them, and I have no pity. They know how to remedy their problem. Oh, wondering about that other 5%? Give "Pinpointing Your Folly" a gander…

[28] This quote is particularly noteworthy for those of you who have experienced the academic disaster which is commonly known as the Science section on the ACT.

[29] Basically, applied defeasible reasoning. That is, the same reasoning you're using when you're using best-answer reasoning. I leave it as practical reasoning here because that's the bigger tent in which best-answer reasoning fits.

In some cases, practical reasoning has to be conducted under conditions of uncertainty in which conditions are changing fast. Here, a weak argument could be a reasonable basis for arriving at a decision on what to do now. The plan can always be revised later as new data come in, but too much collecting of data could mean that the decision to act is useless because too much time has lapsed without any action. (Walton, *Goal-Based Reasoning for Argumentation*, p. 42)

Does that sound anything like your testing day experience? I'll bet it does. Crazily enough, Walton is describing scenarios that range from artificial intelligence programming[30] to Stephen Curry's decision-making process in an NBA basketball game. And you get to turn loose that same form or reasoning on the ACT and SAT. Nice. Ball out.

Now sometimes students get confused about practical reasoning on standardized tests. This confusion stems in part from the fact that in real life people often encounter two types of practical reasoning: instrumental and values/ethical.[31] The ACT and SAT creators will do their best to avoid values-driven or ethical forms of reasoning for their questions, except perhaps on the essays. Thus, bringing a values-based form of practical reasoning into the test would present a unique problem for you. Structurally, you're still reasoning the right way, but your *a priori* assumption would lead you to bring extra information into the test, information that would likely be outside the ACT or SAT's closed world. While it's frustrating (much like a video

---

[30] Practical reasoning models are in part how the computer program AlphaGo beat human champion Lee Sedol 4-1 in five games of *Go* in 2016. They also played a pivotal role in Deep Blue's excellence at chess.

[31] Values/ethical reasoning means stuff that people want to argue about. You know those topics of conversation that aren't supposed to be brought up at Thanksgiving dinner when the whole family is there? Yeah, those involve values or ethics. People care deeply about those topics, but there's a ton of disagreement about them as well. Instrumental practical reasoning is much simpler, like "how do I make it so my stomach isn't growling anymore?" (probable answer: figure out how to get food in my belly) or "how do I score higher on my ACT or SAT?" (ideally this book answers that question at least in part).

game at times), you don't get to control the parameters of the ACT or SAT's closed world.[32] They've attempted to create worlds that involve instrumental practical reasoning only. It's possible that they'll fail on occasion, but that's probably not going to be an immediate concern on your individual test day. Use the instrumental model only for your test day.

Just as a reminder, this chapter (and its first part) contains the most important information this book provides. Get your head wrapped around its lessons and how they apply to your test-day domination. In simplest form, you're merely using elimination as a strategy. But you now know that it goes much deeper than that.

---

[32] I actually ran into this problem in school. I kept missing questions on a multiple choice test, and I couldn't figure out why, since I knew the material inside and out. Once I realized that I was missing questions because I disagreed with my teacher, I just switched my bubbled answers on future tests to what the teacher expected as the answer and walked away with my A. I debated with that teacher *after* I'd received my grade. Sometimes it's advisable to play the game. Since the ACT and SAT don't care what you bubble, I suggest you play theirs (or my modified version of it) if you intend to apply to a college that requires standardized test scores. But that's 100% your call.

"If thou findest in human life anything better than justice, truth, temperance, fortitude, and, in a word, anything better than thy own mind's self-satisfaction in the things which it enables thee to do according to right reason, and in the condition that is assigned to thee without thy own choice; if, I say, thou seest anything better than is, turn to it with all thy soul, and enjoy that which thou hast found to be the best." Marcus Aurelius

"That man is altogether best who considers all things himself and marks what will be better afterwards and at the end; and he, again, is good who listens to a good adviser; but whoever neither thinks for himself nor keeps in mind what another tells him, he is an unprofitable man." Hesiod

"You must know that it is no easy thing for a principle to become one's own, unless each day you maintain it and hear it maintained, as well as work it out in life." Epictetus

"As it is the character of Genius to penetrate with a lynx's beam into unfathomable abysses and uncreated worlds, and to see what is not, so it is the property of good sense to distinguish perfectly, and judge accurately what really is." Hannah More

"One cannot give a recipe for wise judgment: it resembles appropriate muscular action, which is attained by the myriad lessons in nicety of balance and of aim that only practice can give." George Eliot

Chapter 4: Stories of Math

Almost every standardized test loves to ask questions about integers. And a healthy 50% of my students couldn't tell you what an integer might be. You might be among them, or you might be among those who have a general idea but aren't certain you've got it quite right. Never fear: I have a tale for you. It might be tall and it might be true—I've never bothered to investigate. It is a wonderful way to remember the integer, and that's all we need.

In ancient Rome, in the days before Caesar Augustus, the Roman soldiers were generally composed of simple farming folk. When their commanding officer (who probably wasn't of such "common stock") came by to observe the troops, the soldiers would bang on their breastplates and shout "Integritas!" to demonstrate that their armor was sound. For those wondering, yes this is the Latin root for the English word *integrity*, which can mean whole, sound, or unimpaired.

With the ascension of Caesar Augustus to emperor, the dynamics of the Roman military shifted. Now the emperor had his own private group of soldiers, the Praetorian Guard. And then there were the regular soldiers. When the Praetorian Guard tested their armor, they would just shout "Hail Caesar!" The regular soldiers also changed their cry; they now shouted "Integer!" to show that they were whole, sound, uncorrupt (The Praetorian Guard was notorious for killing people and just being shady in general.). So whenever you think of the word "integer," let out a Maximus-like shout and embrace your role as a true soldier. Be a *Gladiator* on the test: be whole, be sound.

Now you're probably thinking, I swear we were talking about math in this chapter. And we are! When we use the word "integer" in math, we imbue it with the same meaning as those steady Roman soldiers. An integer is whole, not corrupted by any fractional, decimal, or other addition. So an integer can be 0, -5, and 500.

Numbers like ½, .65, and $\sqrt{29}$ would not qualify as integers. No one, not even a Roman emperor, can dilute the wholeness of our integers. Boom!

(One small side note: you may want to shout "In-te-ger!" *internally* during your actual test. Just as courtesy to your fellow test-takers.)

Now let's get into the stories. Oh, right, the story *problems*. But, we'll start with a simple problem, one that lacks a real story to it, just for practice. Here's the problem:

If $x^4 = 16$, what does $x^3 - x^2 + 5 = ?$

Screaming yet? This is actually a super simple problem. We just have to do one simple thing: stop reading when we reach the comma that closes off the "if" statement and try to figure out what the test writers have told us. Ready?

If $x^4 = 16$...Hmm, what else can I figure out?

Oh!

Then x must equal 2! Booyah!

Now let's return to that little tricky part from before. You know, the bit after the comma.

$x^3 - x^2 + 5 = ?$

Well, x = 2, so let's try plugging it in

$2^3 - 2^2 + 5 = ?$

$8 - 4 + 5 = 9$

Now do that happy dance. Math loves you.

So here's your new math rule (and this rule holds for reading, science, and any other question):

When you see an **If** statement, stop at the comma that follows the "if" and try to figure out what they've told you up to that point. Only move on once you've figured out the "if" statement.

Let's move on to a fully-fleshed story problem.

Archibald Anchorage just purchased a scone and a coffee for $3.75 from nearby neighborhood coffee shop, but lost his receipt, so he cannot see how much each food item cost. He knows that his friend Alexandra Alexis purchased two scones and a coffee from the same coffee shop for $6.40. Given the information provided, how much did Archibald spend on his cup of coffee?

   A) $1.10

   B) $1.25

   C) $2.65

   D) $2.80

   E) Cannot be determined from the information given.

Words. Words! WORDS! So many words! Ah! There's nothing worse than word problems. Or so it might seem anyway. I remember when I was in school that my teachers used to beat into my head that I had to turn their convoluted stories into algebra. For them, there was no other option. It didn't matter that I could get the right answer another way; it had to be their way. What they never bothered to explain to me was that algebra can be used to both tell and resolve stories, sometimes faster than when using my own methods!

Here's a brief anecdote: about a month after launching QuotEd ACT Science, iTunes Connect (the app developer's backend) reported the total sales of my apps and how much I'd made, but it didn't list how many I'd sold of each app like it normally did! Now at that time, my two apps, QuotEd Reading Comprehension and QuotEd ACT Science, were priced differently in the App Store, so that made a difference in how much I should have made. And because I had only recently launched QuotEd ACT Science, I wanted to know how many copies I'd sold of each app. So what did I do? Well, I suppose I could have waited until iTunes Connect repaired its errant reporting, but I'm not always patient enough to see how long I'll need to wait. So, I instead decided to turn my problem over to algebra to see what I could find out. Oh, you're curious? Tell you what, it's a decent enough story that we'll tackle my iTunes problem at the end of this chapter.

Where were we? Oh yes, words! Here's the thing, if you can read, you can do math. And if you can read and do math, then you can do story problems. Let's set up a rough, extended syllogism just to review:

Everyone who can read is able to do math.

Everyone who is able to do math is able to do story problems.

Therefore, everyone who can read (this book!) is able to do story problems.

Oh yeah, I'm sneaky like that. I just snuck in a syllogism for review and used it as a rhetorical tool to convince you that story problems are not your biggest problem on ACT or SAT math. So let's look at our super scary, coffee shop escapade.

Archibald Anchorage just purchased a scone and a coffee for $3.75 from nearby neighborhood coffee shop, but lost his receipt, so he cannot see how much each food item cost. He knows that his friend Alexandra Alexis purchased two scones and a coffee from the same coffee shop for $6.40. Given the information provided, how much did Archibald spend on his cup of coffee?

A) $1.10

B) $1.25

C) $2.65

D) $2.80

E) Cannot be determined from the information given.

Now, it is possible to backsolve this question (plugging in answers until you find one that works), but I only advocate for backsolving when other methods fail. This is in part because it isn't always the fastest method and in part because the ACT, much more so than the SAT, is constructed to lure you into selecting a wrong answer. If you're diving into the answer choices as your first step, you're well on your way to being swindled by the ACT. Don't say that I didn't warn you. I should say, though, that tutors tend to be split in their opinions on backsolving. So, you'll find others who might counsel you differently. Let's just say those tutors and I would respectfully disagree. Since you're the one taking the test, you get to decide which approach you'll use!

With all of that said, let's get after this question. I'm going to take it apart in two different ways. The first will be an attempt to get after it logically, but without specifically dropping a full algebraic equation. The first way takes a bit longer, but it demonstrates that it's possible to solve this problem without being an algebraic-equation-creation wizard. The second approach will use algebra and is pretty efficient.

Way 1: Archibald has purchased a scone and coffee. Alexandra has purchased two scones and a coffee. Do you see the difference between their purchases? Alexandra has purchased one more scone. That's it. Now, we know that Archibald spent $3.75 and Alexandra spent $6.40. Here's where we have to get our detective hats on. If the only difference between their two purchases is that Alexandra bought one more score, then wouldn't the cost of that scone be whatever was added on to Archibald's $3.75 to get to Alexandra's $6.40? Let's lay it out in a pseudo-algebraic form:

Archibald's purchase: 1 scone and 1 coffee costs him $3.75

Alexandra's purchase: 2 scones and 1 coffee costs her $6.40

Once again, are there any similarities or differences in their purchases? Well, they both had only one coffee (rookie mistake), but it appears that Alexandra was hungrier for scones (I'm guessing they had clotted cream and strawberry jam to go with the fresh scones. MmmMm). Now that we're all salivating over the scones, let's consider what Alexandra's understandable desire for two scones does to her purchase in comparison to Archibald's. Alexandra has one more scone and spent $2.65 more.

Wait, wouldn't that mean Alexandra's scone cost $2.65? Yes! We're done. Answer C. Game over. Drop the microphone—we're going home.

Oh...shoot. The question was about the coffee? Are you serious?! I'll show you a *##^@^#^@ coffee! I did all that work and missed this stupid question, and all I want now is a fresh crumbly scone with rich clotted cream and jam. So lame.

Fine, what's the price of the coffee? Well, Archibald had 1 scone and 1 coffee and spent $3.75. If his scone costs $2.65, then his coffee must have cost $1.10. Choice A. Are you happy now, ACT and SAT?

Way 2 (go?): Algebra Time!

Archibald Anchorage just purchased a scone and a coffee for $3.75 from nearby neighborhood coffee shop, but lost his receipt, so he cannot see how much each food item cost. He knows that his friend Alexandra Alexis purchased two scones and a coffee from the same coffee shop for $6.40. Given the information provided, how much did Archibald spend on his cup of coffee?

A) $1.10

B) $1.25

C) $2.65

D) $2.80

E) Cannot be determined from the information given.

I'm gonna have scones be x and coffee be c. Frankly you could use any letters, but I don't like using s for scones because I have sloppy handwriting and my s looks perilously close to a 5 sometimes. Back to the problem.

Archibald: $1x + 1c = 3.75$

Alexandra: $2x + 1c = 6.40$

There's at least three different moves we could make right now. I'm going to subtract one from the other, but you could use substitution or graph them. Also, I've dropped the number 1 from the front of my variables. Feel free to use it or leave it out. I'm assuming that if you like algebra, you probably don't write the 1 out in front anyway.

$$x + c = 3.75$$

$$\underline{- \ 2x + c = 6.40}$$

$$-x \quad = -2.65$$

So, x = $2.65

Now go back to the question. Do **_NOT_** go to the answer choices! That "not" emphatic enough for you to see? Remember x was our scones, and our question isn't about scones. Our question is about coffee. So, let's find c using Archibald's equation:

$2.65 + c = 3.75$

Subtract 2.65 from each side.

$2.65 + c = 3.75$

$\underline{-2.65 \qquad -2.65}$

$c = 1.10$

Well would you look at that. Choice A is our winner. We've answered the question and no one got hurt.

Now glance at this story problem that uses a (seemingly) crazy ACT formula. These are always fun. Just a heads up, we'll want a calculator for this one.

Oscar is travelling and notices that the temperature reading at a nearby bank is listed as 10° F. Because Oscar is a curious individual, he wonders what the temperature would be if he were to measure the temperature in degrees Celsius. He uses a search engine to find the formula for converting Fahrenheit to Celsius and comes across F = ⁹/₅ C + 32. Given this formula, what is the approximate temperature in degrees Celsius?

A) -12°.

B) -14°.

C)   5°.

D) 32°.

E) 50°.

Ah! Equations! Ah! Even worse, it's an equation that I used once in junior high. Ah AH! Done screaming? Out of your system? Excellent.

When the ACT or SAT gives you random formulas, *do a happy dance!* I mean it. No matter how bizarre the formula, if the test gives it to you, then all you have to do is plop information into the equation where it goes. To be more blunt, you are playing a matching game. Literally. If you could handle *Go Fish!* or *Memory* as a child (or if you can simply match your socks), you should be able to handle this question.

Okay, so they have to give me either F or C. Now I only need to look for which they give me. Ooh, nasty nasty. They gave me *F*, not *C*. This equation is much easier if they give me C, but they don't. Oh well, let's work with what they gave us for the formula.

$10 = \frac{9}{5} C + 32$

Nice, simple algebra time.

$10 = \frac{9}{5} C + 32$

$\underline{-32 \qquad\qquad -32}$

$-22 = \frac{9}{5} C$

Multiply each side by $\frac{5}{9}$ to get rid of the fraction (or multiply each side by 5 and then divide by 9)

$-12.222222 = C$

So the closest to that would be answer A. Whoo! Done!

Compared to your expectations this chapter might be a bit brief. If you take a peek at "Performance-Enhancing Accelerators," I think you'll find ample mathematical resources suggested. I wanted this chapter to explore some of the concepts students struggle with the most. Otherwise I'd have written an entire math book, and this chapter would be 70,000 words and numbers. I want you to reflect on the few ideas and approaches presented here and integrate them into your math studies at school and on your practice tests.

Speaking of school, teachers are one of the greatest support systems you'll have for your ACT and SAT math. Your teachers want you to do well on the ACT and SAT. In fact, this is one time when you are complete partners in your mathematical improvement because they aren't the ones testing you, so they have zero investment in creating that magical bell curve teachers often adhere to. This does not mean, however, that you should simply thrust your official ACT or SAT prep book in front of them and say, "How do I do well on this?" Your teachers would justifiably tell you to pay better attention in class and that they don't have time to teach you an entire four years' worth of math in two weeks to account for everything the ACT and SAT might ask.

As long as you come with specific questions that have stumped you and only two or three of them each day, teachers are usually thrilled to help. Of course, if you're typically a pain in class, this may not be as true. Even in that case, though, most teachers are still willing to help. Teachers can be awesome.

I must note, however, that teachers don't always make awesome partners in test prep. Here's why: they want you to learn a concept and be able to apply it from multiple angles. While they value problem solving, their emphasis tends to be on understanding, which is excellent for classroom instruction. When I taught seventh-grade math, I created my own homework problems and tests so that students were forced to engage with the concepts they needed to learn.

The difficulty with a concept-driven approach is that it often doesn't help with problem-solving skills. I'd note that some of the math programs I see today plunge students into weird applications of the concepts they've just learned, which also tends to impede problem-solving skills. Instead of learning how to solve problems, students learn to fear them and to find peers who were clever enough to figure them out. They don't ask their peers how to become better problem solvers; they ask how they can get the answer.

Even if your school has a problem-solving focused curriculum, it's quite possible that you aren't a world-class problem-solver. Further, teachers prefer a problem-solving approach that involves demonstration and algebra. While understandable, you need the full arsenal of problem-solving approaches at your fingertips if you're to best the test. Plausible reasoning, half-cocked theories that might work maybe, and shortcuts of varying nature—Archimedes wrote most of his proofs with shortcuts. It's okay—are all elements that you must have at the ready in order to handle the fast-paced problems found on an ACT or SAT.

Thus, when you ask your teachers questions, remind them that you'd like to know if there's a shortcut or other way that you can use to swiftly handle questions. Ask if there's a way with the multiple-choice answers to navigate the question in a different way. Remind them that you aren't trying to cheat your mathematical mind or math class. You just wonder if they sometimes have mental shortcuts or ways of getting through problems that they initially can't figure out. Inquire how they handled the math section when they took the ACT or SAT.

So, guide your teachers. They are great helpers for test prep, but remember that they aren't typically thinking in test-prep mode. You have to get them there. I might add that whichever teachers tend to have a sense of humor also seem to have a knack for finding loopholes in standardized test questions. This might be because you need to look for "loopholes" to execute certain jokes or pranks, so that habit of mind is already in place when it comes to finding loopholes on the ACT or SAT.

Remember, if you want to ask teachers for ACT or SAT help, prepare your questions beforehand and think through how you'll get them to introduce you to math shortcuts, should those shortcuts exist.

Now I believe I promised you a story. When my ACT Science app first launched, I only charged $0.99 for it. Even though the hints in it alone would have justified my charging $20.00 for it if it were in book form, there were only forty questions in it on the day I released it. While I was adding questions each day, I didn't think I was justified in charging $4.99 for my ACT Science app when that's what I charged for my SAT and ACT reading comprehension app which had over three hundred questions in it at the time. This meant that my apps were priced differently. Not a big deal.

When you first launch an app, you wake early each morning to check how many of each app you've had downloaded and how much money you've made. Imagine my surprise when I opened up my iTunes Connect account to see what the previous day had been like and all I saw was how much money I'd made and how many apps I'd sold! I had made $199.20 and sold 80 apps. I couldn't tell, though whether I'd sold a bunch of my recently released QuotEd ACT Science or the slightly older QuotEd Reading Comprehension. Had I sold multiple copies of only one of the two apps? If so, which one? Ah! The frustration! Rather than waiting for Apple to fix its flawed backend, I started wondering whether there was any way I could uncover how many of each app I'd sold. I did know how many total apps were sold and the total money from those sales, but that was it.

The difficulty with this problem wasn't so much that it was an algebra problem. The difficulty was that it was a real world problem! You know how in math class everyone likes to talk about real world problems? Well, this was one. I much prefer the "real world" problems given in math class because I know that an answer can be found. I didn't even know if I could find the answer with the information I was given. That comfort blanket of knowing that the problem is in math class (and thus the problem must be solvable) wasn't there. I literally didn't know, which kind of made my head spin.

I had two questions. First, was it possible to figure out how many of each app I'd sold from the information that I knew? Second, was *I* capable of figuring out how to do that? I didn't like that second question at all. I decided to risk wounding my pride, and I dove into the problem. Since I had two apps, the one thing I knew was that I'd need two variables, one for each app. The other thing I knew was that I'd need two equations if I wanted to get answers with these two variables (two variables generally means you need two equations to solve—keep that in mind). Now I needed to combine the numbers that I already had from iTunes Connect with the information that I wanted to find.

Okay, I'll make "a" be my ACT Science apps sold and "r" be my reading comprehension apps sold. Added together, that would make all the apps sold. That means a + r = 80. First equation, easy peasy. But I need a second equation. Ugh. What. All right, let's see. I know how much I earned, $199.20. I also know that I charge $4.99 for the reading app and $0.99 for the science app. I need a second equation and I need dollars. (Come on!) Wait… if I try $4.99r and $0.99a, that would give something that looks equation-like. So maybe 0.99a + 4.99r = 199.20? Whatever, let's roll with this.

$$a + r = 80$$

$$0.99a + 4.99r = 199.2$$

I'm going to get "a" by itself in that first equation.

$$a = 80 - r$$

With a nice and easy substitution for "a" into the second equation…

$$0.99 (80 - r) + 4.99r = 199.2$$

Distribute that 0.99 and then finish solving the problem.

$$79.2 - 0.99r + 4.99r = 199.2$$

$$\underline{-79.2 \qquad\qquad -79.2}$$

$$-0.99r + 4.99r = 120$$

$$4.00r = 120$$

$$r = 30$$

If I plug 30 in for "r" in the first equation, that means that "a" equals 50. Looks like I sold 50 of QuotEd ACT Science and 30 of QuotEd Reading Comprehension that day. Glad I could feed my obsessoin.

Because math quotes are great and I didn't want to pick favorites, I decided to end this chapter with some quick-hitting math hints instead. Try them out!

Math Hints!

1. Draw a picture.

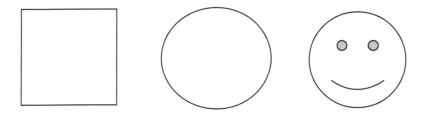

2. If you see an "if," stop at the comma and engage the information given by the "if," then proceed to the rest of the question.

3. When you see an unfamiliar equation, try plugging the given information into the equation. Who knows, you might be able to solve it after all!

4. To avoid careless errors, write out your work on paper *before* typing it into your calculator.

5. Keep moving!

Chapter 5: But This Isn't Science

One of the greatest flaws in the ACT's design is its Science section. To the great misfortune of test-takers, the SAT is attempting to join the ACT in its folly, though the SAT's attempt isn't quite so abhorrent as the ACT's. Making the best of things, this at least gives me opportunity to introduce an old-school SAT analogy to explain my reservations about ACT "science":

ACT Science is to real science :: a veggie burger is to a hamburger.[33]

It might look like a burger, and you can surround it with a bun, condiments, and fried onions. It might even taste great! Nevertheless, none of these is enough to make a veggie burger the same as a hamburger. I recall when my mother tried removing red meat from my family's diet (overall a good thing) and replacing it with meat substitutes (overall a terrible thing). That first bite of a tofu burger made me wish that I could time travel back to before that bite and never, ever experience it again. The appearance was mostly there, but first came the alien texture, which did not interact with the bun and lettuce as expected, and then in rapid succession the simultaneously tasteless and foul-tasting flavor of the tofu burger. In a completely unrelated sequence of events,[34] this was also the only time I have ever doused a burger with both catsup and mustard.

As someone who enjoys a black bean burger now and then (a delicious variation of the veggie burger when done well), I wish that the ACT Science section was half as appetizing, but that sadly isn't the case. Think of the worst veggie burger you've ever tasted,[35] and

---

[33] The "::" should be read "as."

[34] Not really. When your mother comes from a family of Depression-era-raised farmers, Benjamin Franklin's "Waste not, want not," is a mealtime mantra. I managed to choke that mangled impression of a burger down under pain of no dessert (thank the heavens, *not* tofu-based), but never again…

[35] Looking at you, tofu burger.

that's the ACT Science section. Unfortunately for you, there isn't enough catsup and mustard in the world to remedy the ACT Science section, which is the same experience you might have with a veggie burger, now that I think more about it.

Now you might be thinking that the world shouldn't be this cruel. I agree. I can't believe I had to eat a veggie burger as a child.

Oh, were you thinking about having to take the ACT Science section? Yes, I suppose that would fit things as well. I'll tell you a story, though, that will either give me your pity or encourage you to think "um, who gives a rip?".

You see, a number of years ago I started my studies of plausible reasoning models, bits of cognitive psychology, English literacy, and English language learner research. You may remember some of this from the chapters on reasoning. This research kept milling around in my head along with constant experimenting on my students with the various insights from my studies. When you're working with kids from all over the USA and all over the world, the generic advice that you can find online doesn't apply, so you either do your own research or do nothing for your students other than repeat the same advice that doesn't apply.[36] So after much experimenting and even more analysis of my findings alongside those I read about, I finally came up with an awesome app to address the most consistent gaps I found with my students.[37] That app was *QuotEd Reading Comprehension.*

"Wait a minute..." I'm sure you're thinking, "this chapter is supposed to be about science." And so it is. You see, I made that app

---

[36] Sadly, I've had way too many students come to me after working with such tutors. Many times I can't even fit them into my schedule, so I give them quick advice by phone if I have time. Yes, this book exists in part to reduce the number of these phone calls I receive.

[37] My athletes and artists also couldn't pretend they were unable to do all their homework anymore when they went out of town for away tournaments, shows, and camps. They could almost always use QuotEd!

and was ready to rest on my laurels. I mean, I'd made an app that was original to my research; students' scores were improving faster because of it; and people all over the world were downloading it.[38] Touchdown dance.

Then my students started nudging me with "You know a science app would be really helpful *toooo*."[39] I'm sitting there thinking, "I just invested hundreds of hours of research and writing and thousands of dollars in development to create a reading app! A culminating event! And you want *more!* Have you seen *Oliver!*?"[40]

I don't enjoy thinking of myself as a sucker, but somehow my students' begging[41] made me consider their plight. The ACT Science section is dismal, horrible, and unfair. So, even though I swore I'd never make another app after *QuotEd Reading Comprehension* and certainly didn't think I'd ever make anything for a pseudoscience section of all things, I found myself sucked deeper and deeper into the development of *QuotEd ACT Science*. That's right, my students made me create a tofu burger.

So while you might think your lives are bad having to deal with ACT Science, at least you didn't have to go deep inside the messed-up minds of the ACT Science section's creators. I want my life back. Thanks to the pleading of my former students, you benefit by not having to waste your lives repeating the same tormented labors I

---

[38] Seriously. Australians in particular loved it. Someday I'll head down under to find out why.

[39] Though this was preferable to the idiots in bars and elsewhere who kept asking me to create an app for common sense whenever they found out that I'd made an app for reading comprehension. "What you should really make is an app for common sense," guffaw, "because that's what's really in short supply," (face tightening up in despondency about everyone else's lack of common sense). The moral of the story is that no matter how useful something is, someone will always have an idea about what *better* thing you could do (or ridiculous thing, like a common sense app). Please don't be that person. I write this as a reminder to myself as well.

[40] The 1968 musical. The repetition of *"more"* is simply terrifying to any six-year-old whose parents allow him to watch it.

[41] That's a euphemistic way of putting it. It was nagging.

encountered while building *QuotEd ACT Science*. You can simply download the app and use it as indicated in the "Performance Enhancing Accelerators" and "An Outline of Success" chapters. Yeah, the burger still tastes bad, but at least you didn't have to make it by hand, too!

Because the pertinent insights for the ACT Science section can be found in that app, there is no reason to repeat them here. I will, however, add some thoughts which may help you to uncover some individual struggles that the app's specific hints aren't intended to address.[42]

In general, three different types of people experience difficulties with the ACT Science section. Knowing which one you are can be critical if you want to improve your score. Here are the three common types:

1) This student can be an absolutely fantastic reader or a solid reader. But, this student is typically ambivalent or negative about science. Shockingly, there are more of these students than you'd imagine. If your reading score is more than 4 points higher than your science, then you are probably a student who falls into this category.

If you are this student, there are two ways of improving your science score (aside from taking a bunch of science classes in school). First, you need to realize that if you can read, you can probably do science. And on the ACT, if you can read, you can *definitely* handle the science. The ACT Science section is simply a weird reading section,[43] so just apply the reading skills you have to it. I've seen students who were interested in theater – and only theater – perform sensationally

---

[42] As with any form of instruction, you will need to adapt the app's hints to the live ACT Science sections in front of you on test day (and in practice).

[43] There's the occasional "real" science question (I typically warn students to expect up to four each test). Sometimes that question is about which direction gravity works in the simplest of layperson terms (i.e. down towards Earth). Other times that question might be a bit harder, in which case you'll either know it from your studies or you'll have to guess and move on to the other thirty-nine questions you'll have a better chance at.

on the Science section, because they realized that it was a reading test, first and foremost.

Second, you will need to learn how to focus on the important information and learn to not *read* the unimportant information. Now let me be clear, I'm not advocating for an approach that involves skipping certain reading, per se. What I mean is that you have to learn to cut through the scientific jargon to see what's actually going on.

Here's an example of an ACT Science question, one loaded with information that comes from a passage about Lake Erie (I'm leaving out the passage for the sake of space.):

> Each autumn, the top layer [of water] cools, and the wind mixes it deeper and deeper into the bottom layer. Eventually the whole water column is the same temperature, and the wind can again mix it from top to bottom and the oxygen can be restored from the air. In the Central Basin, this phenomenon typically occurs in early to mid-September, when oxygen is restored from top to bottom. Given this information, if the Lake Erie region had an unseasonably warm later summer (August and September), what would likely be the result?

Aside from the fact that the passage might make this a little easier, we don't actually need the passage for our example.[44] Let's take this apart. Water *cools* and *mixes*. Great. Here's what else we need to know: this typically happens in autumn/mid-September. Then, we find out that it has been *unseasonably warm* in August and September for a particular year.

Once you've got this information in place, you should be able to see what inference the test-makers are looking for. Normal situation: water cools with cooling weather. Question's situation: weather is warmer than usual. Any thoughts as to what might happen to that water? (Hint: it's not going to cool!)

---

[44] This will be the case for a decent number of ACT Science questions that have more than one sentence in them. See "General Hints" in *QuotEd ACT Science* for more.

Now here's some jargon that we didn't need to obsess over: oxygen restored from the air, Central Basin, phenomenon, Lake Erie region. We read all of those things, but we didn't really read them, not in the sense that we retained any information that they gave us. Another way of looking at it is that we simply focused on the weather and water warming and cooling. That's the information that we really *read*.

Final thought on the student who falls into type 1: your ACT Reading score shouldn't be more than 4 points higher than your ACT Science score, unless you are typically scoring 35s and 36s on the reading section. Then you might have a 5- or 6-point difference, though 4 points should still be your goal.

2) This student is a big fan of science classes, or at least most of those classes, and has great grades in them too. But this student's ACT Science section score never reflects that interest or apparent ability.

The ACT Science section "measures the interpretation, analysis, evaluation, reasoning, and problem-solving skills required in the natural sciences." (or that's the ACT's claim, anyway). If you like real science but struggle with the ACT's version of science, you will want to recall how scientific reasoning works. For a quick review of the basics, a Google search should get you started.

Beyond that simple yet important refresher, make certain that you are able to negotiate scientific reading. Yes, that includes "just reading graphs" as ACT Science is often unhelpfully described, but it also means comprehending the scientific terms as they are used and defined in paragraphs. To strengthen that skill, you'll have to strengthen your overall reading comprehension. But, that doesn't mean you have to start reading *War and Peace*. Start reading science articles in *National Geographic* or *The New Yorker*. And you can choose whichever ones interest you, though try a few that fall outside your normal interests too!

In a nutshell, if you're a type 2 student, then you'll need to strengthen how well you read the arguments made in the ACT Science section. That's the ACT prep you want.[45]

3) This is a student who struggles with both reading and science. Typically, these students are described as "poor test-takers," but often they are just non-readers, reluctant readers, or students who only read if it's assigned as homework. If you don't read regularly, you will likely test poorly, though there is the occasional exception to this rule. When in doubt, assume you aren't the exception.

Fortunately, most of the advice for types 1 and 2 will help you. But there are additional things you can do.

If you have a few months before your next ACT, try to increase your weekly reading load by 10-30 pages a week. You'll be surprised at how much that can help. Obviously, more than that is better, but life can be busy in high school. Science reading should be your focus, but almost any genre will be of benefit.

If you have only a few weeks, practice reading tables, graphs, and diagrams. The faster you can understand them, the easier the ACT Science section will be for you. And if you only have a few days, well, use *QuotEd ACT Science* to point you to the specific types of questions the ACT asks.

If you can't figure out which type of student you might be, your classroom teachers might be able to give you a clue. If you're working with an ACT tutor or taking an ACT prep class, ask your instructor. A good tutor should be able to help you discern why you're struggling with the ACT Science section. Plus, your teachers or tutors could have some specific suggestions to add to the above from their time with you as a student!

---

[45] I wonder if *The Art of Deception* will offer any assistance with this. Hmmm…

"In other studies you go as far as others have gone before you, and there is nothing more to know; but in a scientific pursuit there is continual food for discovery and wonder." Mary Shelley

Chapter 6: Romancing Your Audience

You have to love your audience. If you write and you don't love your audience, you will be boring. Or worse, you will be incomprehensible.

When I'm explaining something to one of my nieces or nephews, I don't simply look for the shortcuts. If I do, they'll quickly point out that I've left some critical detail out or look at me with quizzical disgust. They don't want their time wasted, and I don't blame them. Of course, if I decide to go on forever about some minutia that isn't critical to what I'm explaining, then they'll either find a way to escape my long-winded narrative or tell me point-blank that they aren't interested anymore.

Now why, you might think, is he droning on and on about these nieces and nephews? Here's why: I do love them. And because I love them, I relish sharing exciting ideas with them (as an example, "exciting" might be how to build a secret tunnel in the basement). I don't want to bore them. My love for them and desire to communicate effectively with them is precisely the attitude your writing and editing need if they are to be consistently excellent.

This brief chapter deals with two types of writing—that which you have written and that which you are editing for someone else. We often find it easier to care about the former more than the latter, but it's still common for people to struggle with caring much for either. We'll deal with your own writing first and then look at editing others' writings.

There's probably nothing harder than loving your SAT and ACT essay readers. I mean, they're paid to spend as little time as possible grading your essay. Not a whole lot to love there. Here's the thing, though, can you imagine if you had their job? They're reading hundreds of essays, many illegible and most poorly written. Also, it's doubtful that the readers are the tenured sort of college professors or top-paid high school instructors. They're reviewing these essays because they need the cash, not for the love of reviewing illegible and poorly-written essays. (There might be a few, oddball exceptions to the above speculations, but that doesn't diminish my point.) There is no dishonor in taking on work because you need the cash (hello there, Alexandre Dumas et al.), but taking on the task of reviewing essays written by disgruntled, dispassionate, disenchanted, and generally just dissing teens? Yikes.

Are you feeling a touch of empathy for those poor essay readers? Now imagine if every essay they were to read was written carelessly and disinterestedly. They'd probably end up cranky and apathetic themselves. Excited to have them read your essays in that mood? I thought not.

So, consider their plight as you craft that SAT or ACT essay. They're tired and looking for a pick-me-up. Your essay can be that pick-me-up.

But you don't just have to be their pick-me-up. If you want your essay to be well received (that is, get a high score), then you'll need to be focused on your audience. Do your ideas connect? Do your examples make sense? Will your audience leave wondering whether they've just encountered the Mad Hatter or a normal human being?

Now if you're wondering, "Hey, where can I find a way to make certain my ideas connect?", it might behoove you to read through *They Say, I Say*, which was mentioned in the first chapter. If you're wondering how you might evaluate others' ideas and how they are presented, then *The Art of Deception* will offer you an excellent starting place.

If you can present a lively engagement of the prompts given to you by the ACT and SAT *and* imagine how your mentally-downtrodden readers might be brought back to life through your writing's zest, then you have a chance of gaining an excellent score. Of perhaps greater import, you will have improved the day of another poor person who is caught in the standardized testing machine: your reader.

So let's have at some ways to engage the ACT and SAT's prompts. We'll go ACT first. This is because the ACT essay tends to befuddle more students than the SAT essay. Why? Well, College Board makes the SAT *and* AP Language and Composition. If you take AP Lang,[46] you'll be at least 90% prepared for the SAT's essay prompt.[47] Pretty smooth business move by the SAT if you ask me. So, we'll tackle the ACT's essay a bit more in depth, just because students in general struggle with it more. Let's start off with a sample prompt:

Most people want to make certain students are learning, and most people believe classrooms should be places of unconstrained learning. However, these two desires are sometimes in conflict. In particular, to make certain that students are learning necessitates the collection of data. Now this data can come in various forms, but once the data is there, it often shapes classroom learning. Given the tension between the desire for free inquiry and knowledge that students are learning, how do we best balance the two values? How should we think about the conflicts of the data-driven school and free-inquiry school models?

Perspective 1	Perspective 2	Perspective 3
Data-driven decisions are the only way we can know that students receive the information needed for 21st century success. Students should not be at the mercy of an individual teacher's philosophies of learning.	The freedom of the individual teacher to meet specific classrooms needs is the most important thing. Data-driven decisions ignore individuals and the distinct culture each learning community has. Data drives out free inquiry.	Data should shape classroom learning, but teachers and learning communities should have the freedom to interpret that data for themselves. Thus, data is a partner for learning communities, not a restriction of their autonomy.

---

[46] The moral of this is, obviously enough, to take AP Lang. Well played, SAT, well played.
[47] Worried about that remaining 10%? Well, remember those books in the "Read" chapter? Yeah, those might be a thing.

Essay Task

Write an essay in which you evaluate multiple perspectives on the conflict between classroom freedom and classroom data. In your essay, please account for the following:

- Examine the perspectives given
- Defend your own perspective on the issue
- Explore how your perspective and those given relate

Your perspective may agree in part, completely, or not at all with the perspective given. Regardless, support your ideas with cogent analysis and relevant examples.

Well… this looks like a treasure of an assignment. Really, ACT? Frankly, given the structure, I just want to go all meta on them and drop some scholastic, Thomas Aquinas-styled argumentation on them. They wouldn't be able to handle our deft philosophizing. They've already set us up for that structure. We'd just be referencing the scholastic structure they've already introduced. Oh yeah. Unfamiliar with the structure I'm talking about? Here's good ol' TA's argumentation structure:

Question at hand (How should we think about the conflicts between the data-driven school and free-inquiry school models?)

Objection 1 (Perspective 1)

Objection 2 (Perspective 2)

Objection 3 (Perspective 3)

On the contrary (This is where we get to start our argument by citing some other authority on the subject. TA would often cite The Philosopher here [aka Aristotle, aka the Stagyrite, aka the logical ton of bricks to drop on unsuspecting people].)

I answer that (Boom, here's our essay with our full perspective.)

Reply to Objection 1 (Here's where we destroy Perspective 1.)

Reply to Objection 2 (Here's where we destroy Perspective 2.)

Reply to Objection 3 (Here's where we destroy Perspective 3.)

Didn't the ACT set us up perfectly for using TA's scholastic structure to write a killer essay? They've already started us off with the question at hand and the 3 objections. I don't suggest actually using his structure, though, because we don't typically use that exact scholastic structure in modern writing.[48] Your ACT readers might be confused by your smooth scholastic stylings, though you could certainly give them a hint that you're dropping some TA knowledge and style on them by using TA in your "On the contrary" instead of Aristotle. Still, we'd frustrate our readers more than guide them if we employed the smoothness of scholastic style, just because that style is a bit unusual today. And remember, we're trying to romance them. Frustration will likely have the opposite effect.

Modern persuasive writing does, however, use a modified version of scholastic structure. In fact, I'm going to give you two such modified models that you can use to respond to this particular ACT prompt, ones which you'll now see have some striking similarities to the scholastic structure you've just seen. The first model is for when you disagree with two of them but agree (or mostly agree) with one of them. The second model is for when you disagree with all of them (or have a distinct point of view that they just don't account for).

---

[48] FYI, you'll probably encounter Thomas Aquinas in a first-year philosophy class in college. You're welcome for the introduction to his argument style. It befuddled me when I first engaged Thomas Aquinas's writing in college, so you're ahead of me at least.

Model 1 Outline

Paragraph 1: Intro Paragraph

Sentence 1: Thesis or qualified thesis (Qualified as in you add a qualifier to it.)

Sentence 2: Either tag-teams with Sentence 1 or further references the prompt

Sentence 3: Organizing sentence (Mostly leads into Paragraph 2)

Paragraph 2: Contending Hypotheses

Sentence 1: Acknowledge relative merits of and then undermine Perspective 1

Sentence 2: Undermine Perspective 2 by connecting it to Perspective 1[49]

Sentence 3: Say what both perspectives miss

Paragraph 3: What I Want to Say, Part 1

Sentence 1: Agree with Perspective 3 (but with your own spin)

Sentence 2: Example that goes with your perspective

Sentence 3: Talk more about your example

Sentence 4: More about your example or add a cousin example

---

[49] Typically, two of the perspectives will appear to be direct opposites. Steal a debater's trick—paint them both as extreme and then you really only have to disprove one of the two. This also allows you to take on the guise of the Aristotelian mean. Now you are the moderate intellectual who will wax eloquently in this collegial discussion.

Sentence 5: Move me (well, to the next paragraph at least)

Paragraph 4: What I Want to Say, Part 2

Sentence 1: Hear me roar (well, hear me muse about more of my perspective)

Sentence 2: Example, baby!

Sentence 3: Tell me how cool this example is

Sentence 4: Close me out or keep going with <u>relevant</u> examples

Paragraph 5: Remember How Suave I Was? Allow Me to Recap

Sentence 1: Hey, remember those extremists? Yeah, glad they're gone

Sentence 2: Party bus to my perspective and its examples!

Sentence 3: Ah yeah, you love my Aristotelean mean

If that general outline is too open-ended for you—though it shouldn't be—you're in luck. Because I'm nice, here's a possible template for you to memorize if you're too scared to organize your own thoughts on test day. You'll be in better shape if you create your own (either in advance or on test day), but I offer this nonetheless:

Model 1 Template

Just about everyone acknowledges that _____ matter(s). Even such acknowledgement, however, accounts for _____only in part.[50] When

---

[50] You may notice that I'm making both Sentence 1 and Sentence 2 into a qualified thesis with this template. My main assertion technically won't appear until later with this modification. My temporary thesis is that extremes might exist. I'll drop my full thesis later after I've warmed my readers up to my casual Aristotelian temperance.

the conversation on _____ is initiated at its extremes, little progress or constructive analysis can be made.

Perspective 1 is compelling enough to consider further, but the overriding assumption that _____ is a problem to be overcome undermines Perspective 1's persuasiveness. Curiously, Perspective 2 appears to be Perspective 1's polar opposite. Now, _____ is treated as the overwhelming problem. In their brevity,[51] neither perspective seems to account for [whatever part of my intended thesis is].

This is where Perspective 3's statement "[literally quote Perspective 3 here]" invites more discussion. Consider [first example]. In X context, [first example] allows for [some relevant positive thing]. If we explore [first example] further, we would find that [some other positive benefit emerges]. These benefits merely begin our discussion of [my intended thesis].

A natural consequence of [my intended thesis] opens up consideration of [second example]. In [some particular scenario that involves the second example], [some fantastic benefit emerges]. While [second example] might be difficult to implement in all cases, measured use of [second example] offers enough advantage that its occasional difficulty is worth navigating.

If we allow the extremes of Perspective 1 and Perspective 2 to dominate our thinking on _____, we overlook so many possibilities. Though our exploration of _____through Perspective 3's lens has been brief, we have already seen inspiring potential in just two examples. _____ should be considered [write Perspective 3's thesis in your own words].

---

[51] The ACT likes to be wowed with "academic" vocabulary. I typically recommend that you find five "money words" that you know really well and can insert into almost any academic debate. I've worked one here into this example as a freebie for you. You're welcome. Also, using "brevity" here demonstrates that you've thought through the fact that maybe the perspectives would seem less extreme if they had been allowed to expand their arguments a tad. Now you seem even more like a measure individual. Look at you, you sophisticated smarty. Welcome to college.

All right, should we put that into play?

Most people want to make certain students are learning, and most people believe classrooms should be places of unconstrained learning. However, these two desires are sometimes in conflict. In particular, to make certain that students are learning necessitates the collection of data. Now this data can come in various forms, but once the data is there, it often shapes classroom learning. Given the tension between the desire for both free inquiry and knowledge that students are learning, how do we best balance the two values? How should we think about the conflicts of the data-driven school and free-inquiry school models?

Perspective 1	Perspective 2	Perspective 3
Data-driven decisions are the only way we can know that students receive the information needed for 21st century success. Students should not be at the mercy of an individual teacher's philosophies of learning.	The freedom of the individual teacher to meet specific class-rooms needs is the most important thing. Data-driven decisions ignore individuals and the distinct culture each learning community has. Data drives out free inquiry.	Data should shape classroom learning, but teachers and learning communities should have the freedom to interpret that data for themselves. Thus, data is a partner for learning communities, not a restriction of their autonomy.

Essay Task

Write an essay in which you evaluate multiple perspectives on the conflict between classroom freedom and classroom data. In your essay, please account for the following:

- Examine the perspectives given
- Defend your own perspective on the issue
- Explore how your perspective and those given relate

Your perspective may agree in part, completely, or not at all with the perspective given. Regardless, support your ideas with cogent analysis and relevant examples.

Just about everyone acknowledges that both educational freedom and data on student learning matter. Even such acknowledgement, however, accounts for the interplay of data and learning only in part. When the conversation on education is initiated at its extremes, little progress or constructive analysis can be made.

Perspective 1 is compelling enough to consider further, but the overriding assumption that teacher independence is a problem that needs to be overcome undermines Perspective 1's persuasiveness. Curiously, Perspective 2 appears to be Perspective 1's polar opposite. Now, student data is treated as the overwhelming problem. In their brevity, neither perspective accounts for the necessary interplay of free inquiry and accountability to educational standards in a democratic society.

This is where Perspective 3's statement that "data is a partner for learning communities" invites more discussion. Consider how data could partner with a middle school teacher's instruction if she has thirty kids in her classroom, as is sometimes the case in urban schools. In that context, regular data on the thirty students would allow the teacher to provide personalized instruction to each student instead of having to teach generically to the group. This personalized instruction offers more possibility for free inquiry for individual students than if the teacher generically implements a course of study for all thirty students. If we explore data in this setting further, we would find that the teacher could also garner an idea of her students' strengths and weaknesses before she even meets them, which would make her preparation time even more specific to those thirty students. These benefits merely begin our discussion of how data can partner with learning communities.

A natural consequence of a partnership of learning with data opens up consideration of how school budgets can be administered. Instead of schools randomly throwing money at different supplemental materials or programs, schools could use data to pinpoint which types of materials have proven most effective for their specific educational needs, saving schools money and improving the education of students. While using data for budgeting decisions might be difficult to implement in all cases, say for programs like music which resist some data metrics, measured use of data for purchasing learning materials offers enough advantage that the occasional difficulty is worth navigating.

If we allow the extremes of Perspective 1 and Perspective 2 to dominate our thinking on educational freedom and data, we overlook so many possibilities. Though our exploration of the interplay between data and learning through Perspective 3's lens has been brief, we have already seen inspiring potential in just two examples. The role of data in learning is that of a partner that can be called upon when data might enhance the teaching and learning experience.

Whew. There we go. Glad that's over. Now is this essay a 6 on all four of the ACT's metrics?[52] I wouldn't give it 6s across the board,[53] but it's at a 4 or above in each category, which should serve our needs. The difficulty with templates is that they can restrict us when we want to craft our writing in a manner more suited to the subject matter. With that said, templates also help us to craft a written response swiftly when we're under a severe time constraint. Since I'm not in the room with you to discuss whether you'd benefit from this template or not, you'll have to decide for yourself or try some practice essays out and have someone else grade them.

If that's what our template looks like in action, let's see what our outline can generate. I'll utilize it without naming the perspectives in my essay, which is a safe approach for skilled writers. I will also avoid using the word "I" to make this essay even less like my prior one, even though I'm taking the same argument.

While data collection in education should certainly be large-scale so that educational trends can be observed, any insights gained should be implemented at the local level alone. The local level would include school boards, schools, and individual teachers.

Now some might argue that the local level will be unqualified to interpret the data in the local context, but this view holds an untested assumption: that data-driven decisions coming from a national or state overseer will more effectively merge large-scale data with the small-scale idiosyncrasies of each individual learning community. To acknowledge the small-scale idiosyncrasies of each learning community is not the same as promoting each teacher to become ruler of his or her own fiefdom—no

---

[52] Ideas and Analysis, Development and Support, Organization, and Language Use.

[53] I never came back to my line about educational standards in a democratic society. Instead of acting as an assertion full of promise, it now sits unaddressed in judgment on my essay. Don't leave important lines dangling.

one is truly asking for a feudal system that ignores the essential friction of democratic debate.

That essential friction encourages freedom of inquiry without creating a reinvention or reworking of the wheel. With independent macro-data driving decisions, education will simply find itself making the same wheels over and over again, though certainly with a new paint job. With independent micro-data driving decisions (i.e. data derived from individual teacher analysis alone), education will not have remade the tire part of the wheel; rather, it will have patched and re-patched the same tire ad nauseam. When the friction of debates over data and learning is permitted, however, fresh insights from macro-data sets can invite teachers to invent new learning opportunities for their unique classrooms.

Expanding the idea of education to include the local school board and school leaders, though, offers the most hope for a beneficial resolution of the conflicting ideas of teacher independence and data-driven learning. While it may not be fully possible for a local community to mediate the conflict between national data trends and local teacher insights, at least a modicum of progress can be made as the local community engages in conversation about the eccentric pedagogical approach of a certain Mr. Smith and that approach's connection to state or national educational conversations about learning outcomes. More importantly, the local community can dialogue about how relevant some of those large-scale trends are to the immediate educational context. Including teachers within that dialogue but not limiting it to teachers alone would create the parameters for a reasonable amount of teacher freedom that is mediated by the local educational community as a whole.

Rather than pushing the conversation about data and freedom of inquiry to its extremes—and ignoring the other local stakeholders all the while—an earnest debate about the constructive interaction teachers and data can have is a realistic ideal. National-level educational data can and should inform local teaching, not to deny teacher freedom, but to ensure that teachers can freely choose how to engage that data in conversation with their local community.

Do you feel Aristotelian? Are teachers free and yet connected to their local communities? You know, if I had time to edit this, I think I could make that case.[54] As it stands now, the third paragraph is the

---

[54] Because I typed this one, I gave myself less time than you have. And aside from a

one that leaves this essay's overall thrust in question. I'm not digging my analogy. It's the kind of insertion that seems brilliant in the moment,[55] but afterwards you're just left with regret.

I should note, by the way, that you can adapt the template or outline. If I were writing the essay with stylistic flourish intended to demonstrate how I truly *feel* about this topic (if I happen to have feelings about it), I would heavily modify my own outline. The basic Aristotelian argument pattern would now be buried beneath anchoring elements that I'd interweave to make certain that my reader's mind would be stuck reflecting upon them (at least as best I can) and thus reflecting upon my argument which is hidden behind them. It could go something like this:

"Welcome to the data-bot. You're now entering a world where the algorithm will guide your learning for your optimal result."

"Hello, children! This is a cheery place where you can let your minds explore. Come, be free, and learn what you will."

At first glance, those two statements would appear to have nothing in common. Indeed, I think I'd choose the second statement for my educational experience if I were given the option. The first statement seems eerily Orwellian, so I think I'll pass. Cheery place, here I come!

If a second pass is taken at those statements, however, you'll find that they are both algorithmic in essence. The first statement is obviously so, but the second statement is implicitly so. Algorithms are merely a set of procedures or a single procedure. At

---

quick edit or two, I did not polish these essays into perfect form. Why? It's because you won't get to polish yours. So why should I present you with examples that I've polished? Seems like cheating to me, particularly since I created the outline and template for you to use. You will notice that for both the template and outline that I made small adjustments as I was writing to make them fit to how my mind was framing each particular essay.

[55] I'm pretty sure I tried using this analogy at least once in college with a midnight essay deadline. Maybe not, but then it was a similar one. Pro tip: don't try a clever reworking of a cliché in the middle of the night unless you have time to look it over and edit it the next day. Your cleverness may appear madness by morning...

their simplest, they are intended to help a machine repeat the same outcome or produce a desired outcome. Both the data-bot and the cheery place intend to repeat a same outcome for their learners. The outcomes for the data-bot algorithm and the outcomes for the cheery place algorithm are different outcomes to be sure, but each algorithm has a distinct set of goals for its outputs. If a teacher's input is "do what you will" (though what you will is still influenced by that individual teacher), then there is a certain output engendered by that input. So while the two statements differ in their inputs and outputs, they are both algorithmic.

The question, then, is about how we should view this algorithmic nature. Do we want a learning environment where every inch of the learning experience is some data-fed algorithm? Do we want a learning environment where the whim of an individual can determine the education of a multitude?

Once again, a similarity between the statements appears. If education is data-driven, isn't some individual (or the still-individual output of group-think) determining what data are important and how that gets tossed into the algorithm? How is that strikingly different from an individual teacher determining what a group of students learn? Indeed, both statements are eerily dystopian in their own ways. While the first might be Orwellian, the second could be straight out of *Brave New World*.

The common element in the two dystopias alluded to is their top-down control. One is on a macro scale, the other a micro. For a learner, neither scale provides the optimal algorithm. To keep the hobgoblins of dystopian horrors from our democratic society, the tension between data-driven decision making in education and individual classroom freedom for teachers must remain. Not only is this tension representative of the tensions inherent in a democratic society, but it also offers students the possibility of avoiding a truly dystopian education. The creative tension of national, state, local, and individual teacher demands can foster a deep yet novel education for each learner, one that, if still algorithmic, will at least be more interesting.

I'll be honest, I'm not certain about this essay. I was going for a full-out romancing of my audience here. I'm pretty sure they weren't bored initially,[56] but I don't know if I managed to keep anyone

---

[56] Actually, you're my audience right now. Were you bored? Or were you momentarily intrigued? This is the third essay you've read on this topic now. Did it

awake. Discussions of algorithms can bog down quickly, and this one did. Strangely enough, I use just enough jargon that this essay obtains the semblance of meaning. If my reader finds my opening and conclusion intriguing enough *and* I get the three-minute-or-less grading special (typical of the ACT), I may luck into a high score, even though I personally don't think this essay is too strong.[57] Since it almost sounds smart, I may just get by.

That seems like enough time spent with Model 1. Model 2, if you recall, is for when you disagree with all of the perspectives given (or have a distinct point of view that they just don't account for). If you like one of the perspectives, use Model 1. If you don't like *any* of the perspectives, employ Model 2 for their quick dismissal. Below is Model 2's outline for your perusal.

Model 2 Outline

Paragraph 1: Intro Paragraph

Sentence 1: Track A is a thesis /Track B is a "hook"[58]

Sentence 2: Track A is an extension of a thesis/Track B is a transition into a thesis

Sentence 3: Track A is an organizing sentence for the essay/Track B is a thesis

---

wake you up after the last two snoozers? Feeling any sympathy for the poor saps who will be reading your ACT essays now? Oh yeah, I'm sneaky like that.

[57] Though I snuck in an Emerson allusion, all while remaking it into an entirely different thing. Bonus points? Maybe if I get an Emerson fan as one of my readers. I can hope, right?

[58] The "Track A/Track B" distinction means that you can do one or the other. So Track A is thesis statement, sentence extending thesis, sentence organizing essay. Track B is hook, transitional sentence, thesis statement. Please don't try both simultaneously because it won't make sense.

Paragraph 2: Contending Hypotheses

Sentence 1: Other perspectives exist, but they exhibit some weaknesses

Sentence 2: Acknowledge, then undermine Perspective 1

Sentence 3: Undermine Perspective 2 by connecting it to Perspective 1

Sentence 4: Chuck Perspective 3 under a Mega Bus

Sentence 5: Discuss how all the perspectives are limited or remain wanting

Paragraph 3: What I Want to Say, Part 1

Sentence 1: Here's a delimited perspective

Sentence 2: Example that goes with your perspective

Sentence 3: Talk more about your example

Sentence 4: More about your example or add a cousin example

Sentence 5: Move me (well, to the next paragraph at least)

Paragraph 4: What I Want to Say, Part 2

Sentence 1: Hear me roar (well, hear me muse about more of my perspective)

Sentence 2: Example, baby!

Sentence 3: Tell me how cool this example is

Sentence 4: Close me out or keep going with <u>relevant</u> examples

Paragraph 5: Remember How Suave I Was? Allow Me to Recap

Sentence 1: There exist a multitude of perspectives

Sentence 2: But party bus to my perspective and its examples because they're the best!

Sentence 3: Okay, a bit more calmly, but yeah, my perspective rocks[59]

All right, that's enough time with the ACT. I know we've tatted Aristotle all over the ACT's prompts, but even his appearance isn't enough to keep me in ACT-land. Let's change over to the SAT. This time, a sample passage for you to try your hand at will appear at the end of my brief discourse on approaching the essay.

I had an instructor at Oxford University who was famous for crossing off the introductory paragraph to every single essay students wrote. Each time, you'd receive a gigantic "X" through the very paragraph you'd invested the most time in and a note with an arrow pointing to your second paragraph with the directive: "start here." As someone who believed his introductions were often the best part of his essays,[60] such directives were demoralizing.

I didn't know what to do. I was, however, quite sick of losing points on each essay and seeing that infernal red "X" through my glorious introduction. So on my third essay, I wrote the whole thing like I

---

[59] I hadn't intended to include these models (or the sample essays) because I already told you to get a copy of *They Say, I Say*, which will more than prepare you for the prompts. Then I had a student who told me, "Yeah, I know, but I just can't figure out how to deal with their viewpoints *and* address what I want to say," so I wrote her Model 2's outline on the spot. She adapted it to her own uses, calmed down, and rocked her essay. Because you have *They Say, I Say* readily at hand, I'm not giving you a template for this model, just the outline. You can design your own template using *They Say, I Say* if you're that paranoid.

[60] Yes, this likely does say something about the quality of those essays. With that said, I recall many a person who fell to that pen.

normally did, but then right after I'd finished proofing the whole thing, I deleted my introduction. This time the instructor[61] loved the essay.[62] No red "X." Boom.

Now you might be wondering why I've bothered with this story about introductions. Is this one of those stories that I just have to tell everybody and couldn't imagine leaving out of my book? While I remember indignantly retelling the story in college, I don't know that it's a regular in my storytelling Rolodex these days. I mention this story because I've had a number of students who can't figure out how to get into their essay. One possible way of dealing with that problem is to simply write your essay without an introduction. Start your essay with a point you wish to make about the passage you've had to read. Then move on to another point. Write as you know how, just without that introduction. Your essay will survive without it.

For those of you who just can't get over the idea of not having an introduction, there are two other solutions. The first is almost as easy as having no introduction: give your essay a title. There's your intro. The second is not as easy because you have to write an introduction of some nature. Let's say the passage you were supposed to analyze was basically an extension of one of my footnote diatribes railing against the ACT.[63] All you need to do is

---

[61] In case you're wondering why I write "instructor" instead of "professor," you don't typically call someone "professor" at Oxford unless they have a chaired professorship, which is a distinguished position. So even though my instructor had a doctorate, "instructor" (or tutor or lecturer) fits better. Weird, I know.

[62] Well, actually, my instructor liked it so well that I was accused of plagiarism. One line in the essay demonstrated a depth of insight (and writing skill) that my instructor thought was beyond my abilities. I still don't know whether to be insulted or flattered by this. Fortunately, I was able to show that yes, in fact, I had written that line and I did have the chops to know what I was talking about in this instance (opera and Greco-Roman mythology? Oh yeah, that was 100% my bailiwick. I'd literally spent my summer prior studying just that. Yes, I'm actually serious. If you want to know why, that's probably a long, in-person conversation. All we need here is a fist pump and "Huzzah!").

[63] Let's be honest, the SAT might actually try to find a passage that does this, given its bitter market share war with the ACT; but only if that passage successfully painted the SAT as the one true test of college readiness, of course. I don't honestly

write something along the lines of "Offering a predominantly negative opinion of the ACT, Kreigh Knerr crafts an argument filled with innuendo, personal anecdote, alliteration, and critical analysis of the ACT's own claims."

It would be crazy awesome if you got to analyze a passage that specialized in innuendo. Of course, innuendo isn't exactly considered the best ground for measured academic thought, so I doubt you'll find it in the passages the SAT selects for you. Fortunately for me, this book isn't supposed to be an academic treatise on the validity of psychometricians' assumptions about college readiness, so innuendo is my sword.

Judging from SAT sample essays, it appears that of the three categories your writing will be evaluated on—reading, analysis, writing—analysis will be the hardest category for gaining perfect or even strong scores. Each category will be scored between one and four points. You'd have to work pretty hard to score below a two on the reading: those are practically given away. I'll give you a quick list of what you'll need for a strong essay in each category:

Reading: Literally tell your reader what happened in the passage you're supposed to analyze. Support this telling (but *don't* replace it) with textual evidence. You can quote from the passage or paraphrase it. But seriously, even if you struggle with your writing skills and have no idea how to do analysis, you can still score reasonably well in reading if you explain the main point and its supporting arguments.

Analysis: I'm going to list a few helpful terms below, but the most important thing here is to both list *and* explain what you see going on. This is your "I see what you did there" moment. You'll get half credit for listing what's going on. For full credit, you need to explain

---

think it would happen, but I'm not throwing the possibility out the window. The SAT wants to be back to number one again. Maybe the SAT's staff watched the indelicate South Park episode involving Bono?

(and provide textual evidence for) what's going on. It's almost impossible that you will actually belabor a point. Belabor away.

While there are many others you can put into play, here's a starter list of some helpful terms you can use to "look smart" on certain SAT essays:

Alliteration—when multiple words start with the same sound in a sentence or paragraph and establish some semblance of unity. Also, a writer's favorite and least favorite tool. Smooth alliteration adds a connective element to writing; overly clever alliteration is irritating. Alliteration (and approximate alliteration) is also the primary weapon in the tongue-twister's arsenal: "She sells seashells down by the seashore." It's almost impossible to write without some alliteration, which means you can find it in *every single SAT passage you examine.* Alliteration is always there. Use it in your analysis if you can't find anything else. It's a freebie for those of us who struggle with analysis.[64]

Allusion—when someone makes an allusion, that person is making an indirect reference to somebody or something. For example, there's an excellent essay titled "The Algorithmic Self"[65] by Frank Pasquale in the Spring 2015 edition of *The Hedgehog Review* which gives subtitles to its various subsections. One of these subtitles is "Repeating Ourselves to Death," which is an allusion to Neil Postman's celebrated cultural criticism *Amusing Ourselves to Death.*[66]

---

[64] Because I'm sometimes absent-minded, I left alliteration out of this chapter's first draft, even though the omnipresence of alliteration in most writing is what inspired this list in the first place.

[65] After you've read the "Private Training" chapter in this book, go ahead and read "The Algorithmic Self." I have probably half my students read it these days and almost every single student preparing for the PSAT. I should note that it's *way better* in the printed magazine form, just because formatting with the pictures makes the read more engaging, but the essay is interesting and excellent enough in any form (particularly the opening three paragraphs, which exhibit some skills that even Stephen Booth of *Precious Nonsense* fame would enjoy).

[66] I'd actually suggest reading Postman's *Technopoly* over *Amusing Ourselves to Death,* but either work is worth exploring. Postman's works are a bit longer, though, so you

Of course, only people who are aware of Postman's book would get the allusion, but that's pretty much the nature of allusions.

Anecdote—this is a fancy way of saying story. Typically it's used in the context of a *personal anecdote*, which just means personal story. I used a personal anecdote earlier when I talked about my Oxford essay-writing experience to introduce the idea of writing without an introductory paragraph.

Argument from authority (appeal to authority)—almost every SAT passage you'll be required to analyze will include some reference to a specific authority and most will include multiple authorities. If you want to drop some knowledge (aka look pretentious), feel free to write *argumentum ad verecundiam*, which is the Latin form. Frankly, you can just write, "Author X enhances her argument's thrust by including outside authorities on the matter. Y and W combine to support author X's argument that this [specific thing in her argument] is important."

Metaphor—when *The Smashing Pumpkins* sing "The world is a vampire," you've got yourself a metaphor, and a dark one at that. Or there's the classic TLC song, "Waterfalls," that a Starbucks barista once serenaded me with when she learned that I'd had eight cups of coffee that day (I'm normally a one-to-two-cup guy): "Don't go chasing waterfalls / Please stick to the rivers and the lakes that you're used to."[67]

If you want more terms, talk to your English teachers, read *The Art of Deception*, take AP Lang, or explore the internet. Remember, this is a starter list, though you could probably handle a whole essay with it alone.

---

may struggle to squeeze them in on top of your ACT and SAT preparations.

[67] Of course, she just meant that I was going to be in the bathroom all night, not that I was chasing the wrong sort of lasses. It was a cruel joke to twist the metaphor to another use like that. Though, I have to give her props. When I was up all night thanks to my overly-caffeinated brain and body, I kept chuckling (and wincing) at her pun.

Writing: Here's where you show off your fancy pants prose. If you haven't gained anything from all the books I recommend in the "Read" chapter or your high school classes, at least remember to present a sense of your style (personality) and the semblance of a structure for your essay. Those are the basics. I've suggested enough resources for the rest that I think you can figure this one out.

Speaking of figuring things out, let's give you that SAT essay prompt so you can practice:

As you read the passage below, consider how Agnes Repplier uses

- evidence, including facts or examples, to support claims.

- reasoning to develop ideas and to connect claims and evidence.

- stylistic or persuasive elements, such as word choice or appeals to emotion, to add power to the ideas expressed.

Adapted from Agnes Repplier, "Words." 1893.

"Do you read the dictionary?" asked M. Theophile Gautier of a young and ardent disciple who had come to him for counsel. "It is the most fruitful and interesting of books. Words have an individual and a relative value. They should be chosen before being placed in position. This word is a mere pebble; that a fine pearl or an amethyst. In art the handicraft is everything, and the absolute distinction of the artist lies, not so much in his capacity to feel nature, as in his power to render it."

We are always pleased to have a wholesome truth presented to us with such genial vivacity, so that we may feel ourselves less edified than diverted, and learn our lesson without the mortifying consciousness of ignorance. He is a wise preceptor who conceals from us his awful rod of office, and grafts his knowledge dexterously upon our self-esteem.

Men must be taught as if you taught them not,
And things unknown proposed as things forgot.

An appreciation of words is so rare that every body naturally thinks he possesses it, and this universal sentiment results in the misuse of a material whose beauty enriches the loving student beyond the dreams of avarice. Musicians know the value of chords; painters know the value of colors; writers are often so blind to the value of words that they are content with a bare expression of their thoughts, disdaining the "labor of the file," and confident that the phrase first seized is for them the phrase of inspiration. They exaggerate the importance of what they have to say, lacking which we should be none the poorer, and underrate the importance of saying it in such fashion that we may welcome its very moderate significance.

For every sentence that may be penned or spoken the right words exist. They lie concealed in the inexhaustible wealth of a vocabulary enriched by centuries of noble thought and delicate manipulation. He who does not find them and fit them into place, who accepts the first term which presents itself rather than search for the expression which accurately and beautifully embodies his meaning, aspires to mediocrity, and is content with failure.

The felicitous choice of words, which with most writers is the result of severe study and unswerving vigilance, seems with a favored few who should be envied and not imitated to be the genuine fruit of inspiration, as though caprice itself could not lead them far astray.

Other writers, never to be confused with those gifted of felicitous choice, test the fortitude of the reader when they choose words whose sense is inadequate to the sound, and whose sound muddies the sense. "All freaks," remarks Mr. Arnold,[68] "tend to impair the beauty and power of language;" yet so prone are we to confuse the bizarre with the picturesque that at present a great deal of English literature resembles a linguistic museum, where every type of monstrosity is cheerfully exhibited and admired. Writers of splendid capacity, of undeniable originality and force, are not ashamed to add their curios to the group, either from sheer impatience of restraint, or, as I sometimes think, from a grim and perverted sense of humor, which is enlivened by noting how far they can venture beyond bounds.

There is a kind of humorousness which a true sense of humor would render impossible; there is a species of originality from which the artist shrinks aghast; and worse than mere vulgarity is the constant employment of words indecorous in

---

[68] Matthew Arnold, a nineteenth century English poet and cultural critic.

themselves, and irreverent in their application, the smirching of clean and noble things with adjectives grossly unfitted for such use, and repellent to all the canons of good taste. This is not the "gentle pressure" which Sophocles put upon common words to wring from them a fresh significance; it is a deliberate abuse of terms, and betrays a lack of that fine quality of self-repression which embraces the power of selection, and is the best characteristic of literary morality.

Authors who are indifferent to the beauties of reserve charge down upon us with a dreadful impetuosity from which there is no escape. The strength that lies in delicacy, the chasteness of style which does not abandon itself to every impulse, are qualities ill-understood by men who subordinate taste to fervor, and whose words, coarse, rank, or unctuous, betray the undisciplined intellect that mistakes passion for power.

Write an essay in which you explain how Agnes Repplier builds an argument to persuade her audience that word selection should not be overlooked. In your essay, analyze how Repplier uses one or more of the features in the directions that precede the passage (or features of your own choice) to strengthen the logic and persuasiveness of her argument. Be sure that your analysis focuses on the most relevant features of the passage.

Your essay should not explain whether you agree with Repplier's claims, but rather explain how Repplier builds an argument to persuade her audience.

And with that, let's turn to a different side of writing.

Editing another person's writing presents a quite different scenario. In the case of the ACT and SAT writings that you must edit, you don't even know their authors. On the one hand, this is wonderful because you can freely critique the essays without feeling like you're being mean to someone else. On the other hand, the essays are often terrible and critique given to the individual might serve that person well.[69]

I often joke with my students that the ACT and SAT expect you to have the grammatical instincts of a copy editor for *The New York Times*. The joke is only partial. The tests expect you to know many of the foundational grammatical elements that dictate *AP Style* and other writing style manuals that control writing standards in different professions. If you'd like to work in those professions at some point or find advancement in your career in a different profession, it's likely that you'll need to know these foundational grammatical elements. While you might complain about this reality—and many do—it is nevertheless a reality.

Note that I didn't suggest in any of the above that you need to be a copy editor or necessarily have those skills in order to find success writing in various fields. I did, however, say that the ACT and SAT expect you to have the instincts of a copy editor. That's a very key point. Success on the ACT English or SAT Writing and Language sections depends on your ability to morph into a copy editor.

A great copy editor knows how to flit between one of two primary tasks: mechanical editing and substantive editing. You will be tasked with expertly navigating both tasks within the same essay but not typically on the same question. Mechanical editing includes knowing which rules (or preferences) your particular publisher prefers. In the ACT and SAT's case, for example, they believe in using the serial comma.[70] Substantive editing (content editing) includes making stylistic changes to the writer's work to fit the rest of the essay (or to fit with the publisher's preferences). Both editing types appear with

---

[69] My editor may have taken this idea a tad too deeply to heart during this book's editing process. Your reading experience is the better for it, though! The remaining horrors within this book's pages were my own pigheaded selections or oversights, including the decision to include a dialogue in the second and third chapters.

[70] *AP Style*, however, does not use the serial comma. Since you're taking the ACT or SAT, learn what a serial comma is. It's easily found online *and* in your Strunk and White grammar book.

regularity, but mechanical editing is usually the easier of the two types for students to markedly improve. This is because mechanical problems of punctuation, for example, are fairly easy to learn, even though high school English teachers often don't teach them.[71]

Substantive editing involves catching three primary things: the style of the essay as it's presently written (*not* how *you'd* write it), the larger context of the essay that your modification will affect, and most importantly the specific question you've been asked. Most students miss the substantive editing questions because they pick an answer choice that they like without even acknowledging the style of the essay they're reading or the question they've been asked to respond to. This includes many excellent readers and writers. I don't know why they do this. If you'd like to perform well on these questions, *make certain you've answered the questions you were asked*!

Now, answering the question you've been asked might seem demeaning to your intelligence. I don't know why it might seem this way, exactly, but I've known more than a few students who felt like their intelligence had been insulted by having to respond to a direct question.[72] Perhaps they've been taught that the only questions that matter are the ones they themselves have created. Even entrepreneurs, though, who are perhaps the most celebrated in present day for their "original thinking" and abilities to "reframe the question" have to respond directly to others' questions at some point, whether they are from employees or from that key customer who will finally make it so their company has actual sales (you know, how you actually have a business instead of just an expensive idea or hobby). Most people don't end up as entrepreneurs, however, so they

---

[71] This might be because when they do, students ignore the lesson anyway. It isn't until an ACT or SAT has punched a student in the face that he'll typically start caring about grammar.

[72] Now, if you feel like your intelligence has been insulted because you're editing essays that look like they were crafted by a 6th grader, I feel your pain. This is supposed to be a college-readiness exam, and you're looking at a 6th grade report on fishing. I get it. I'm bored with these passages, too. Don't let your boredom lead you to sloppy mistakes, though. These sections aren't easy unless you're acing them. Then you can tell me they're easy.

have to respond to specific questions from bosses or people they supervise with even more regularity.

Learning to read or listen to questions well is a sign that you care about the other person. Or simply that you respect that person. It's a good life skill to have if you intend to help people or persuade them to your point of view, which would include romance, of course. You cannot romance another person without taking stock of what they enjoy and value, necessitating that you listen to that person's questions. Even if you don't intend to romance every person around you (probably wise), if you want to flourish in any working environment that involves other people, learning to read well and listen well will provide you with at least one skill that may help you reach that goal.[73]

For the ACT and SAT, answering the question they've asked sums up your task. Most skilled writers and generally excellent test-takers struggle with this idea because they hate the ACT and SAT's sections so much that editing them is just painful. Get past your irritation. Answer the specifications of the question asked. Is this stupid? In many ways, yes. But it is the unfortunate reality of the test. Score well, get a college degree, and you too can expose the standardized tests for their inability to be college or career aligned.

Since the test scores still matter right now, however, you need to play within the constraints of the game the ACT and SAT write. You can use the rules against them, but there isn't a way to operate outside of them completely, no matter how desirable that would be. Answer the question, and help your 6th grade authors sweep their teachers off their feet with their wondrous junior high prose. Remember, you're a copy editor who is trying to help your *writers* romance *their* audiences. It just so happens you are editing for 6th grade writers. Help those awkward souls woo their audiences.

------

[73] Knowing what you're doing helps too. Though if you don't, you can always ask your own questions!

"The state of mind of a writer is not the state of mind of his reader. The writer knows his ideas, and has spent much time with them. The reader meets these ideas for the first time, and must gather them in at a glance. The relation between two ideas may be clear to the writer, and not at all clear to the reader." Garland Greever and Easly S. Jones

"Unity means oneness. A sentence should contain one thought. It may contain two or more statements only when these are closely related parts of a larger thought or impression. A writer should make certain, first, that his thought has unity; and second, that this unity will be obvious to the reader." Garland Greever and Easly S. Jones

"The best argument for a succinct style is this, that if you use words you do not need, or do not understand, you cannot use them well. It is not what a word means, but what it means to you, that is of the deepest import. Let it be a weak word, with a poor history behind it, if you have done good thinking with it, you may yet use it to surprising advantage. But if, on the other hand, it be a strong word that has never aroused more than a misty idea and a flickering emotion in your mind, here lies your danger. You may use it, for there is none to hinder; and it will betray you." Sir Walter Raleigh

"Remember that the object of writing is not the covering of so much blank paper, nor the stringing together of syllables; it is the transference from the author's brain to other people's brains of certain thoughts and situations and sensations. And the best writing is that which conveys, by the simplest and most direct means, the clearest reproduction of the author's ideas." Flora Klickmann

Chapter 7: Performance Enhancing Accelerators

For some of you, this might be the most exciting chapter. Up till now, I've laid out some groundwork for the tests, but I obviously haven't been able to cover every single nuance of the tests. And if I were to do that, you'd be looking at a thousand-page volume. For some reason, I can't imagine anyone hauling that around. So I decided against writing a book no one would use.

Also, I've never been interested in reinventing the wheel. If there's a resource out there that's as good as one I can create or even 90% as good as one I can create, I'll simply use that resource and modify it as I see fit. Only a tutor with an outsized ego or a very specific need creates new products. I've created two that were needed, but I have no desire to duplicate someone else's excellent work just so I can put my own name on it. Plus, some of these resources are even available for free, which I think is fantastic.

Let's dive into the resources that can drive you to even greater testing success. Before we dive in, please keep this in mind: you should study with materials created by the test-makers themselves. Why? Imitations always miss something. They might miss only 5%, but that can become significant pretty quickly for most people. Also, imitations sometimes *add* stuff, which can be worse when it's done accidentally.[74] Who wants to study more than is actually on the test?

I'll split the resources into ACT-only, SAT-only, and helpful-for-both-tests categories.

---

[74] Sometimes tutors add stuff to their materials for a specific training purpose. That's understandable, but you still need real materials from the test-makers so that the training translates over to them.

ACT Only

The Real ACT, 3rd Edition

There are only three full tests in *The Official ACT Prep Guide, 4th Edition*[75] (seriously, ACT?! You can only manage *three??*[76]), but at least they come with explanations. You can see my comments in "An Outline of Success," but the *third edition* is the one you'll actually want, not this most recent edition. We'll cover how to study from it later, but this is your starting text. Also, you want the third edition published by Peterson *not* Wiley. This makes an essential difference.

ACT Question of the Day

Makes sense this would help, right? I won't belabor this. You will need to sign up on the ACT's website for the weekly email of questions.

QuotEd ACT Science

Yeah, this is my app. Did you think I wouldn't list it here? It's got 90% of the strategies I teach my students, and the remainder can easily be pieced together from this book and common sense. This is what you would call a training tool, but it does imitate a subsection of the ACT passages. It's a $5 app that has over 240 practice questions,[77] a full strategy guide that you can use in partnership with *The Real ACT, 3rd Edition*, and a glossary of terms if you'd like to

---

[75] I can't tell you how much it amuses me that the ACT decided to change its title from *The Real ACT Prep Guide* to *The Official ACT Prep Guide* for its 4th edition. I mean, could you copy the SAT anymore? The two test-makers crack me up. They keep imitating each other in ever-tightening spirals. Pretty soon they'll be indistinguishable.

[76] For all the crap I give the ACT, whoever is running its Twitter account quite kindly gave me this information prior to the book's publication. Kuddos to the ACT for a swift and professional response. That was appreciated. I wish that the information given had been that there were five practice tests, but at least I knew to expect three.

[77] That's more than six practice tests' worth of questions. Or to put it another way, that's a $30 book in a $5 app.

freshen up your science vocab (or learn some random geology terms the ACT likes to test). A quick note: the strategies for double passages apply to graphs, tables, and diagrams as well—just section those off as if they were double passages.

SAT Only

The Official SAT Study Guide

There are only four tests in *The Official SAT Study Guide* (ugh), but there are explanations in it at least. The explanations are the long-winded variety (i.e. no shortcuts), but at least they are in the book.

SAT Question of the Day

Once again, it should make sense this would help. Official material from the official test-makers.

Helpful for Both Tests

QuotEd Reading Comprehension

This is my beast-mode training app. Aside from being built of your worst nightmares, this little intellectual puzzle will ramp up your reading comprehension so that ACT and SAT reading will feel like child's play. Of at least equal importance, this app will assist your mind's shift into best-answering reasoning mode.

QuotEd's App for SAT Math

Why didn't I italicize this? Because I'm still deciding on its name. It won't be released until late summer 2016.[78] If, however, you'd like to join my beta testers (and therefore get it for *free*), shoot me an email

---

[78] You're finding this out before the press. Isn't that exciting?! Yeah, probably not. And if the press happens to read this book too, then you won't find out before them. But you'll at least find out before your friends who haven't read my book!

with a copy of your receipt for this book. I am cutting this offer off after the first 500 folks, only because my team[79] can't process more feedback than that. This app will be most helpful for students preparing for the PSAT and SAT, but it will provide help for the ACT as well. Also, this app will pair awesomely with the next book. I won't call twinsies because they aren't *that* similar, but we'll call them partners in crime.

PWN the SAT: Math Guide, 4th edition

This book is simply ridiculous for both ACT and SAT. I love that Mike, the author, took until February of 2016 to release it for the new SAT.[80] Unlike all the clowns who released their study guides in June of 2015 or by early fall, Mike sat there and digested every single nuance of the SAT. It takes a while to get yourself so deep into the minds of the test-makers that you know their assumptions as well as they do. It takes further mastery to figure out how to train others for where those assumptions lead and include shortcuts that will help speed up a student's navigation of the test. Yes, it says SAT; we'll get to why ACT momentarily.

I will say that if you're scoring under an SAT 550 or ACT 23 on math, this book is not for you, at least not until you've worked with some other materials first.[81] But, if you're looking to improve your score significantly and your score is in the mid-500s or above (or mid-20s or above), *PWN the SAT: Math Guide* will be your best study

---

[79] Oh yeah, I'm working with math teachers, professors, and tutors for this one, including one who has directed the math tutoring center at a local university. Why? Because I want it to meet my students' needs, and that includes yours.

[80] Okay fine, I was a little bit annoyed because it forced me to develop some of my own materials and pull from some other awesome materials, but we'll get to that in a moment. Related, I get paid to do my own research and work, so it's not like I had to have Mike do it for me. That's what lazy or incompetent tutors do when they purchase some name-brand book off the shelf without knowing whether its research makes sense or not.

[81] Fortunately, QuotEd's math app will still help because it has elements that will help people with crazy low scores and crazy high scores. *PWN* is intended for high scorers only, though, and does an awesome job of assisting them.

companion because it approaches the SAT thematically (as any top-tier SAT tutor would approach it) and directly references questions in *The Official SAT Study Guide*.

For SAT usage, see the "Outline of Success" chapter on how to use it in your studies. With that said, the book has its own suggestions for its use, so if you need to cram your *PWN* study into a different timetable than this book outlines, you will find that Mike can help you out there. Bonus: if you buy his book, you can email Mike with questions about problems in the book and from real SATs. Boom!

I'll note one thing, though. *PWN the SAT* and I have a decent disagreement on how much you should use the answer choices. I say use them as a last resort because I've seen way too many good math students get wigged out by looking at the answer choices first. Using the answer choices is occasionally an invaluable problem-solving step, but my experience with students has shown me that scanning answers leads to mistakes. There's a better than decent chance that students will see the answer to Step 1 of a *two-step problem* and stop there.

For ACT usage, you might be wondering why on earth I've suggested an SAT book for the ACT. Well, it's because the ACT and SAT math sections become more alike with each passing test. Because the ACT doesn't announce its changes,[82] it's hard sometimes

---

[82] Dear media, please stop skewering the SAT for *announcing* its changes and maybe look at the ACT's shady alterations of its test (and publication of a guide that doesn't match its own, barely-announced, "updated" test for *a whole year!*), which are almost never announced and just sprung upon students! Seriously. And I'm particularly looking at you, coastal journalists. When more people are taking the ACT than the SAT and yet you skewer the SAT alone *all the time*, even when the ACT is featured in the same critical studies as the SAT, you are first ignoring reality and second propping up the ACT's market share because the absence of a critique makes it seem like the ACT is hunky-dory when you're so busy heavily critiquing its nearest competitor exclusively. Do your jobs instead of writing your childhood narrative or whatever causes you to discuss the SAT only. Your wealthy, "helicopter parent" readers and viewers care about both tests. Promise. You'll still get eyeballs if you investigate the ACT, too. I get skewering the SAT, I really do. I still remember one of

to predict every nuance the test will incorporate, but the core elements are relatively the same from test to test. As I mention above, you have to be super careful with *PWN the SAT*'s adherence to backsolving and plugging in, but you also need to learn how to use those skills. While backsolving and plugging in can seriously mislead you on the ACT if they are your first instincts, you do need them as instincts for the occasions that your initial approach to a question fails.

The book is scaled on the hard side, so don't get too overwhelmed if the harder problems are blowing your mind. They are the problems that kids who should regularly be pumping out 36s would find easy. If you're trying to improve from a 25 to a 30 or from a 30 to a 34, you should find some of the problems difficult. That would be how you learn to handle difficult problems. Unfortunately, students don't learn mathematical problem-solving skills at most high schools. This is in part because people (teachers, parents, peers, etc.) often give the impression that math is a realm of natural skill and that pure deductive logic and inductive and defeasible reasoning need not apply. I'd suggest these people take a glance at George Pólya's ideas about mathematical problem solving (more on those momentarily). Returning to our ACT discussion, you can skip the "Measures of Central Tendency and Variability" and "Designing and Interpreting Experiments and Studies" subsections if you're pressed for time. Those aren't typical of ACT math (yet...). Otherwise, have at! Just remember that this book is scaled *hard*. You should feel beat up by it, unless you're already kicking out 35s and 36s on your practice ACT math sections.

The Art of Problem Solving, Volume 1: The Basics

What's that you say, you want more math because you're obsessed

---

David Coleman's comments about vocabulary that was elitist and frankly anti-learning, so I'm not exactly a fan. Skewer away. But don't leave the ACT out of that party.

with that perfect 800 or 36?[83] All right, you little weirdo, I've got you covered. This animal was built for those insane kids who like math competitions. What's great is that the first four chapters will give you insight for improving your mental math operations (you know, the stuff you'll need for the SAT no-calculator section) and also cover some serious levels of math lunacy to help you on your ACT and SAT. Order the teacher's key as well so you'll have explanations. This book is straight HGH. Basically, this book takes *PWN the SAT*'s comparatively gentle touch and cranks it up to immediate torment (headaches galore!). I love this book, but you've probably gathered by now that there's something wrong with me, as all my students realize by their second session at the latest. Anyway, only the first four chapters are needed for ACT and SAT problem solving. Those are ample overkill.

How to Solve It

First, *do not* pick up this book unless you've taken calculus. Second, I mostly put this book here because Pólya is awesome. You see, the whole emphasis that *PWN the SAT* has on "nimbleness" is just a layman's term for what Pólya describes as mathematical plausibility. This whole book is a baby treatise on plausible reasoning and mathematical problem solving.[84] Why do you think a company based on *the Art of Problem Solving* is even a thing? Here's the person who can introduce you to the reasoning models (habits of mind, if you will) that underpin the approach *PWN the SAT* and *the Art of Problem Solving* are trying to fix in your mind. I personally love this book

---

[83] Honestly, if you're using real tests for practice, QuotEd's math app, and *PWN the SAT*, you are absolutely in shape for scoring perfectly without needing any further study. This book is overkill on the difficulty. I'm not saying you should use this book. I'm just giving you one of the resources that I'll use with some students, including my perfect math scorers.

[84] No really, he has four more volumes on the subject. Also, his estimation of a competent high school math student and everyone else's estimation of a competent high school math student happen to be worlds apart. Just keep that in mind if you read him. There's a reason Pólya Problem-Solving Seminars are held at Stanford University, not your local high school (though I mean, that *would* be awesome. Who's in with me?!).

because Pólya undercuts so much of mathematical education as it's taught today. He's all about flawed reasoning at the outset of solving a problem, because that reasoning might lead you to something surer as you work your way through a problem. He's also all about reflecting upon and understanding your past work, whether you "got it right" or missed the problem on your first attempt, because that's how you can grow as a problem solver. You don't need this book, and I've only used it with two of my one-on-one students (who complained about it weekly), but you'd be hard pressed to find a more interesting read on how mathematical problem solving is improved. Plus, you'll be able to march around with a strange looking book; and, when inquirers (who might include your math teacher) raise an eyebrow at so simply titled a book, you can say, "Um, it's Pólya" as if that explains everything.[85]

The Complete Guide to ACT English, 2nd Edition

Whoa… A non-math book?! What?!! Indeed. *The Complete Guide to ACT English* gets the job done if you struggle with the nuts and bolts of English grammar.[86] Unfortunately, most schools ignore standard written English thanks to philosophical objections (merited or not).

---

[85] The reason people love Malcolm Gladwell so much is that he makes them *feel* smart, as if they now know something other people don't know. I think he's a great writer, but I don't think he unravels unheard of worlds, that is unless you were to dive into his endnotes and read every single study or article he cites. *Then* you might indeed find something novel, or at least learn which questions you might ask Mr. Gladwell about how he reached his grandiose conclusions. Now why do I mention Gladwell here? Because if you read Pólya, you might actually become a better problem solver, which means you would truly be smarter instead of just feeling like it. Go Pólya. (Fun fact: one of my former students has done two Pólya Problem-Solving Seminars at Stanford and remarked to me how shocking it was to note the improvement in problem solving from one seminar to the next. To me, that's awesome stuff. I was also amused because that student's never actually read anything *by* Pólya…)

[86] Or if you ignored your English teachers when they taught you grammar. Or if your English teachers are lame and refuse to teach you grammar because it's boring and you should already "know" it. (Or if they're idiots who still adhere to the antiquated whole language learning theory that has so many gaping holes in it that you should have a homophone swap to better describe the theory. Yeah, them's fighting words. Bring it on teachers who are hurting their students with idiocy and arrogance.)

While students in those schools might not share those objections, those students get no say in what they are taught. So, things get a bit rough when you're being tested on standard written English (how people write in most college settings) but you haven't been exposed to a single rule or norm of standard written English. This is where *The Complete Guide to ACT English* becomes your best friend. It unpacks the rules of standard written English precisely as they are tested on the SAT. It isn't the most engaging of reads, but that's not why you use it. You use it because it will improve your score (and maybe your writing in college, too).

Now with all of that said, the author made her name on the old SAT's English section, and she rocked at it. All of her other books fail to live up to the reputation she justifiably built with that first book. I don't like her new SAT English book at all (thus why I've recommended her ACT English book for both tests), and this book is anything but complete. First, the answer key is logically bizarre in its organization. Even when you get used to it, it's still counterintuitive. Second, and more importantly for your studies, this book will either be unhelpful or actually harmful to your performance after page 199. It's great up until that page and then... *Do not use it past page 199.*

Basically, if you struggle with usage and mechanics (punctuation and so on) and the Strunk and White isn't quite enough to turn you into a paranoid copy editor, then *The Complete Guide to ACT English* should meet your needs. If your struggles involve rhetorical skills, namely the reorganizing of paragraphs or adding/subtracting of information, this book is not worth your time. Focus on *They Say, I Say* and the questions you observe in real ACT English or SAT Writing and Language tests and you'll be much better off. Also, this book is about as boring a read as you'll find, because grammar.

Khan Academy

I personally don't enjoy this site most of the time. It is, however, great for a free resource and helps you with at least one way of solving a problem. There are worse options. I'd use this for both SAT *and* ACT prep, at least for math help.[87] It's probably helpful for grammar as well, but I'd be skeptical of its usefulness for reading comprehension.

The YUNiversity

If you like jokes and you want to improve your grammar and vocabulary skills, go to *The YUNiversity* and get lost in its awesome ridiculousness. Also, follow the Twitter feed.

Vocabulary.com

Do you like apps and websites for your training? Well, *Vocabulary.com* is your new best friend, if you weren't already aware of it. Go there. Train hard. Become a wordsmith. Vocab does factor into both ACT and SAT performance. The more words you know, the easier the tests will be. Use this app and website and become a better reader.

That's the list. I trust it's short enough to be helpful but long enough that you found at least one resource you hadn't even heard of. Again, the bulk of those resources are supplemental, so even if you don't use all of them, you can still score well.

---

[87] Yes, I realize that the ACT just partnered with Kaplan. I'll pass.

"The experts themselves are not in the least certain who among them is the most expert." Walter Lippmann

"The importance of reading habitually the best books becomes apparent when one remembers that taste depends very largely on the standards with which we are familiar, and that the ability to enjoy the best and only the best is conditioned upon intimate acquaintance with the best."
Hamilton Wright Mabie

"We want philosophers, among other reasons, because the world is full of false philosophy. The way of experience is beset on every hand by a multitude of verbal judgments, of empty phrases, of word-copies, which pass themselves off as the real thing, which pretend to do duty for concrete fact and, by force of their number and importunity, capture our attention and cause the true originals to be overlooked." L. P. Jacks

Chapter 8: Pinpointing Your Folly

You have to own your mistakes. Any tutor worth her salt will tell you that the mistakes you make in practice are the mistakes you'll make on the test. No, adrenaline will not save you, not on a test that is over two hours long.

Here's the thing. Adrenaline can help and will help, but it won't turn you into a superhuman test-taker. You have to be close to that level *before* adrenaline can take you over the top. To do that, you have to own your mistakes.

So here's your new mantra: I'm an idiot.

Not very uplifting, is it? It's definitely not a Google "genius hour" pat on the back. But standardized testing isn't about being a genius: it's about being your run-of-the-mill accountant, quality control engineer, or lawyer. Success is not screwing up. It's that simple. You'll need creativity on three questions max, but even if you miss those three questions, you can still generate an Ivy League-caliber score. Creativity is nonessential for standardized-test success.

So are you done being a genius?[88] Good. Let's get back to this idiot assumption. You obviously aren't the village idiot, or you wouldn't be reading this book. In fact, you could be a genius; it's just that it won't help you much on your ACT or SAT. So, assume you're an idiot, and let's see what that assumption leads to.

First, find a pattern. Do you miss every grammar question which involves a bunch of words shoved between the subject and verb? Note that and mark <u>each</u> subject-verb mistake as a subject-verb mistake. And then look over those mistakes once a week.

---

[88] If you prefer, we could call you a special snowflake. You need to be done with that, too.

Do you freak out when crazy equations or weird symbols appear on Math or Science tests? Note every single one of them and literally label them as "crazy equations" or whatever shorthand you prefer.

Perhaps your habitual misses are the NOT questions on the ACT. Maybe they are tone questions. Know thyself and know thy weaknesses. Keep looking for your consistent misses and find your error pattern.

Sometimes students exclaim, "But I can't find a pattern!" Well, sometimes your errors won't create a pattern. They will simply appear random. To paraphrase Animaniacs, "Hellooooooo Idiot." Glad you could join us.

Random errors are the hardest to overcome. One of my former students had been working with a tutor prior to working with me, and she was consistently stuck scoring 28s and 29s on the Math section (and the other sections). When we started working together, she was so frustrated because her errors appeared random at every turn. Apparently her tutor agreed with her assessment that there was no commonality among her misses. This is the particular difficulty of identifying the consistency among random errors—they seem random. But really, they aren't.

Your errors are either habitual in the sense that they represent a common theme that I've already mentioned (e.g. not reading the word "NOT" on the ACT) or they are common in the sense that you have a pattern of careless errors. The difficulty with careless errors is that they seem patternless.[89]

Ready for your pattern? Repeat after me: "I. Am. An. Idiot."

---

[89] For this particular student, the pattern was that she consistently was misreading the math questions. Sure, one question involved geometry and the other algebra, but the pattern of the error (misreading) was consistent across the majority of her mistakes. She improved her overall score to a 35, so I'd say she figured out error pattern.

If you go into the test thinking you are smarter than it, you are increasing your odds of screwing up. But if you assume that you are an idiot, you have a fighting chance. If you prefer a softer sounding mantra, try "I'm a moron." It works about the same.

I always joke with my students that I test my best when I'm feeling under the weather. Of course, they look at me in disbelief, but it's actually true that I test better when I'm not feeling that well. "Why would that make any sense whatsoever?" I'm sure you're wondering.

It's a reasonable reaction. But you see, I study and teach tests pretty much all day, every day. So when I'm taking a standardized test, my mindset is "I know your tricks."[90] The problem is that while I do know the underlying thinking that creates a test, that doesn't mean I'm immune to human carelessness. Contrary to what my students believe, I'm not a testing robot. Thus, any hint of intellectual hubris from me, and I'll find myself with a 35 here or a 1590 there.

When I'm a bit under the weather, though, I *know* I'm susceptible to the test-maker's trickery. This self-knowledge forces me to remain, as I like to say, "technical." Relying on technique means that I approach every inch of the test with the knowledge I possess of it. I'm focused on any mistakes I commonly make, any nuances of phrasing the test typically exhibits, and any quirks that I'll have to adjust to mid-test.

Technique in its most specific sense means that I'm relying on the mental approach espoused in chapters two and three. When I'm overconfident in my abilities, my brain reverts to finding that "right" answer. When I'm unwell, or remind myself that I can be an idiot, then I remember my technique and go hunting for the worst answers.

Oh, and lest you think my sidebar tale of testing well when I'm under the weather is hogwash, I once had a student take her ACT

---

[90] If you caught this allusion to *A Night at the Roxbury*, well, you've stumbled upon some cult-classic *gold*.

with a fever of 102°F. Her score still went up two points. Even I would have stayed home sick that day,[91] but she's definitely the poster child for my phrase, "Technique first, brain second." Assume you're an idiot and place technique above your brain.

I'm going to launch into a brief diatribe here. I almost made a whole chapter out of this, but I didn't think an extended version of it would benefit your studies. However, if I leave this topic unmentioned within the pages of this book and particularly this chapter, then I'm doing you a disservice.

American culture markets a "can-do" mindset that anyone can learn. Yet we've somehow permitted a pernicious rumor to overwhelm our reason and ideals and establish itself as a near-sacred truth: some people are just poor test-takers. This rumor is a favorite of students, parents, and teachers alike. Of course, there's probably an equal number of students, parents, and teachers who regard the "poor test-taker" label with suspicion, but their voices aren't typically the ones highlighted by the media. The problem isn't, of course, that the term "poor test-taker" is entirely inaccurate; the problem is that such categorizing of an individual is disabling instead of empowering, misdiagnosing instead of constructive, and misleading instead of clarifying. Simply put, we unhelpfully focus on the symptom instead of the myriad possible causes—causes which can almost always be addressed.

Now, I'm not using the term "disabling" to describe those diagnosed with learning disabilities (see next paragraph), but rather those who are readily equipped to succeed on tests but have been newly bestowed with the title "poor test-taker." It is true that they are now impoverished, but it is only by their acceptance of such an intellectual stigma. Their past poor-testing performance is much

---

[91] I'm not a doctor, but I'm pretty sure a 102° fever is one you don't leave the home with, unless it's to see a doctor.

more likely the result of incautious reading (the capitalized word "NOT" remains a favorite for students to ignore), learning gaps (what's a misplaced modifier?), poor advice (yes, from parents, bad tutors, peers, *and* teachers), or some combination of the above. But if you call someone a poor test-taker, that person no longer has the need to exercise grit, reason, or curiosity—you've told them that all further work is at best marginally helpful because they are just "poor test-takers." For this intellectual enfeeblement alone, that phrase is loathsome.[92]

That is not, however, the only unhelpful element of the poor test-taking brand. I've had students over the years who, when they were little, had various difficulties with reading or other academic skills. Because they were either in private schools or in settings that couldn't provide them with external testing, those students fought hard to succeed in school without ever knowing that they were working so hard in part because of an undiagnosed learning disability. Once those students were tested and provided with proper instruction for managing their respective learning disabilities, it was remarkable to see how much better many of them performed. There are obviously students for whom diagnosis and training do not resolve their every testing difficulty, but those concerns almost always involve situations where standardized tests are not the principle academic concern anyway. As an additional note, while not always categorized as a learning disability per se, test anxiety is a subset of performance anxiety, and its pressure can be debilitating on tests and in life. Learning that you have performance anxiety and then discovering ways of limiting its effects early on is much more helpful than simply shrugging off your performance anxiety because you're a "poor test-taker" and then discovering the joys of dealing with your performance anxiety on the job.[93]

---

[92] Even though, yes, its far-reaching shadow generates a significant marketing advantage for my company and the standardized test prep industry as a whole.

[93] This would be sarcasm, as thick as I can make it. Performance anxiety is not joyous. Yes, some nervousness on test day is good, but true performance anxiety can be debilitating. I would note that few of my students have actually suffered from debilitating performance anxiety. The majority of my students who have struggled

The phrase "poor test-taker" is also problematic when it comes to national conversation about standardized tests themselves. Instead of turning our gaze to the potential deficiencies of a question or an entire test, there's a lazy dismissal of tests as biased against poor test-takers.[94] So instead of critiquing a test like the ACT for specific flaws—and it has many—we are left with a dismissal that sounds more like sour grapes or ignorance than logical reasoning or even common sense. While there might be good reasons for ridding ourselves of standardized tests, the mythological and omnipresent poor test-taker is not a persuasive enough person to support most such arguments, particularly in the cases briefly mentioned in the last two paragraphs. But sometimes people do test poorly because of a poorly-crafted test question, and *that* is far more worth investigating than chalking up a poor testing performance to one's innate poor test-taking abilities.

So instead of dwelling on the pathetic plight of the so-called poor test-taker, let's turn our focus to the plethora of causes for the poor test-taking brand. If someone is testing poorly, ask "Why is that?" instead of branding that person as a poor test-taker. The symptom exists, but it exists because of one or several causes. Those things that cause people to test poorly are what matter. Pinpoint your folly; don't mask it with the lazy brand of the poor test-taker.

Pinpointing your folly doesn't just mean thinking, "I'm an idiot," though. Pinpointing your folly also means that you stop blaming everyone else in your life (parents, teachers, friends) for your shortcomings.

Look, everyone has been shortchanged in life, some more than others. I can list at least fifty ways in which life has given me a raw

---

with nervousness have found that they could channel it productively on test day. Nerves tell you you're alive, which is good in the early morning of your test day!
[94] Which, again, are defined however is convenient for the person talking to you.

deal. I'll bet you can too. But there's a difference between knowing the limitations you have experienced and harping on them as if they controlled your future. They don't, unless you let them. At some point, you have to take ownership of your own life, acknowledge where you are, and figure out what it will take to be where you would like to be. That's what this book is partly for, to give you a road map. I can't help where you've come from, and neither can you, but we can help where you go to.

Here's what I want you to do. Close this book and look up J. A. Adande's November 19, 2014, story "Spurs' fortitude fueled title run." Go read Gregg Popovich's quotes. All of them. But particularly note his quote about how our response to things that don't go our way matters. There's a reason the San Antonio Spurs exhibit consistent excellence. Yes, they have great players. Aren't you a great student or a great learner? I mean, you've read this far into my Donnie Downer chapter. But even great players benefit from an excellent culture. Now go get inspired by Gregg Popovich. The rest of this chapter can wait.

Done reading Adande's article? Good stuff, eh? When I work with my students, I always tell them to trust the process and trust themselves. Their job is to peak on test day. The week before their test is the most important week, sure, but the work they've put in over time is what matters. They are ready to do combat with the ACT or SAT.

I tell all my parents and students that I expect my students to take the test *twice* after working with me. Why? Well, I don't expect my students to be testing robots. I've already mentioned my student with the insanely high fever, but I have had teenage couples breakup literally the night before the test,[95] as well as homecomings and

---

[95] Really? You couldn't wait *twelve hours* to break up? Seriously?! I once refused to take on a student because he had broken up with another one of my students the night before her ACT a few months prior to his asking me to work with him. I figured if he was that inconsiderate of her, I had no interest in working with him. Be a decent human being. Don't dump your significant other the night before a major

proms, family struggles, and all manner of oddities the night before the test that disrupt my students' performances.

My goal for my students is consistent excellence. I don't want you to have to take the test ten times to reach your desired goal, but I don't expect you to hit one specific score every single time.[96] When one of my students scored a 36 this year on his ACT, I kept reminding him that we were just looking for consistent excellence. I would have been fine with a 34, 35, or 36. I say the same to my students who are trying to improve from a 12 to a 16 on the ACT or an 1100 to a 1400 on the SAT. Trust the process; trust your work; keep pursuing excellence.

That's the whole reason for pinpointing your folly: you're trying to reach consistent excellence. Figure out how you tend to be an idiot. Focus on the little things that will help you remedy those follies. You know your mantra. Now use it and be excellent.

---

event. Suck up your anger or pride or whatever and wait twelve hours. Cheers and thanks, The Universe.

[96] The ACT, SAT, and universities don't either. That's why they group scores into testing bands (a possible range of scores that an individual would likely score within).

"How is it possible to expect that mankind will take advice when they will not so much as take warning?" Jonathan Swift

Chapter 9: Private Training, Part 1

I figure it's only fair that I take you through my favorite "training exercise." If you haven't figured it out by now, I think like a personal trainer, only for your brain. We can call this a superset. I typically save this work until my students are absolutely stymied and unable to make further improvements. But, since I'm guiding you through a book, I'll put it here in Chapter 9. Remember that you've been warned. If your mental muscles don't hurt after this chapter, then you're either a candidate for a perfect score or you didn't follow the directions. Just like with lifting weights, follow the advice of your personal trainer if you want to make gains and avoid injury.

So here's how we're going to handle this. I want you to read the selection below with no guidance. Wrestle with it. Try to make sense of it. Use some of the tools you've already seen in *Tips from the Top*. Once you've finished reading, I'll take it apart with you two different ways. First, I'll do a big picture reading, which will be how you'll read 90% of ACT and SAT sections. Then I'll show you how to fight your way through truly dense tests—line by line in some places, cruising along in others.

Alexis de Tocqueville. *Democracy in America*. 1840.

"Chapter VIII: The Principle Of Equality Suggests To The Americans The Idea Of The Indefinite Perfectibility Of Man"

Equality suggests to the human mind several ideas which would not have originated from any other source, and it modifies almost all those previously entertained. I take as an example the idea of human perfectibility, because it is one of the principal notions that the intellect can conceive, and because it constitutes of itself a great philosophical theory, which is every instant to be traced by its consequences in the practice of human affairs. Although man has many points of resemblance with the brute creation, one characteristic is peculiar to himself—he improves: they are incapable of improvement. Mankind could not fail to discover this difference from its earliest period. The idea of perfectibility is therefore as old as the world; equality did not give birth to it, although it has imparted to it a novel character.

When the citizens of a community are classed according to their rank, their profession, or their birth, and when all men are constrained to follow the career which happens to open before them, everyone thinks that the utmost limits of human power are to be discerned in proximity to himself, and none seeks any longer to resist the inevitable law of his destiny. Not indeed that an aristocratic people absolutely contests man's faculty of self-improvement, but they do not hold it to be indefinite; amelioration they conceive, but not change: they imagine that the future condition of society may be better, but not essentially different; and whilst they admit that mankind has made vast strides in improvement, and may still have some to make, they assign to it beforehand certain impassable limits. Thus they do not presume that they have arrived at the supreme good or at absolute truth (what people or what man was ever wild enough to imagine it?) but they cherish a persuasion that they have pretty nearly reached that degree of greatness and knowledge which our imperfect nature admits of; and as nothing moves about them they are willing to fancy that everything is in its fit place. Then it is that the legislator affects to lay down eternal laws; that kings and nations will raise none but imperishable monuments; and that the present generation undertakes to spare generations to come the care of regulating their destinies.

In proportion as castes disappear and the classes of society approximate—as manners, customs, and laws vary, from the tumultuous intercourse of men—as new facts arise—as new truths are brought to light—as ancient opinions are dissipated, and others take their place—the image of an ideal perfection, forever on the wing, presents itself to the human mind. Continual changes are then every instant occurring under the observation of every man: the position of some is rendered worse; and he learns but too well, that no people and no individual, how enlightened soever they may be, can lay claim to infallibility;—the condition of others is improved; whence he infers that man is endowed with an indefinite faculty of improvement. His reverses teach him that none may hope to have discovered absolute good—his success stimulates him to the never-ending pursuit of it. Thus, forever seeking—forever falling, to rise again—often disappointed, but not discouraged—he tends unceasingly towards that unmeasured greatness so indistinctly visible at the end of the long track which humanity has yet to tread. It can hardly be believed how many facts naturally flow from the philosophical theory of the indefinite perfectibility of man, or how strong an influence it exercises even on men who, living entirely for the purposes of action and not of thought, seem to conform their actions to it, without knowing anything about it. I accost an American sailor, and I inquire why the ships of his country are built so as to last but for a short time; he answers without hesitation that the art of navigation is every day making such rapid progress, that the finest vessel would become almost useless if it lasted beyond a certain number of years. In these words, which fell accidentally and on a particular subject from a man of rude attainments, I recognize the general and systematic idea upon which a great people directs all its concerns.

Aristocratic nations are naturally too apt to narrow the scope of human perfectibility; democratic nations to expand it beyond compass.

Now that was fun, right? A little rough? Okay, let's do this! Time to see how we can mark it up for overall comprehension.

Alexis de Tocqueville. *Democracy in America*. 1840.

"Chapter VIII: The Principle Of Equality Suggests To The Americans The Idea Of The Indefinite Perfectibility Of Man"

<u>Equality suggests</u> to the human mind several <u>ideas</u> which would <u>not</u> have <u>originated</u> from [any other source], and it <u>modifies</u> almost <u>all</u> those <u>previously</u> entertained. I take as an example the idea of human perfectibility, because it is one of the principal notions that the intellect can conceive, and because it constitutes of itself a great philosophical theory, which is every instant to be traced by its consequences in the practice of human affairs. Although man has many points of resemblance with the brute creation, one characteristic is peculiar to himself—<u>he improves</u>: they are incapable of improvement. Mankind could not fail to discover this difference from its earliest period. [The idea of perfectibility is therefore as old as the world; equality did not give birth to it, although it has imparted to it a novel character.]

One possible summary: human perfectibility an example for equality's role in human mind.

When the <u>citizens</u> of a community <u>are classed</u> according to their rank, their profession, or their birth, and when all men are <u>constrained</u> to follow the career which happens to open before them, everyone thinks that the <u>utmost limits</u> of human power are to be discerned in <u>proximity to himself</u>, and none seeks any longer to resist the inevitable law of his destiny. Not indeed that an aristocratic people absolutely contests man's faculty of self-improvement, but they do not hold it to be indefinite; amelioration they conceive, but not change: they imagine that the future condition of society may be better, but not essentially different; and whilst <u>they admit</u> that <u>mankind</u> has made <u>vast</u> strides in <u>improvement</u>, and may still have some to make, <u>they assign</u> to it beforehand certain <u>impassable limits</u>. Thus they do not presume that they have arrived at the supreme good or at absolute truth (what people or what man was ever wild enough to imagine it?) but they cherish a persuasion that they have pretty nearly reached that degree of greatness and knowledge which our imperfect nature admits of; and as nothing moves about them they are willing to fancy that everything is in its fit place. Then it is that the legislator affects to lay down eternal laws; that kings and nations will raise none but imperishable monuments; and that the present generation undertakes to spare generations to come the care of regulating their destinies.

One possible summary: aristocratic societies (class-based societies) limit people.

In proportion as castes disappear and the classes of society approximate—as manners, customs, and laws vary, from the tumultuous intercourse of men—as new facts arise—as new truths are brought to light—as ancient opinions are dissipated, and others take their place—the <u>image</u> of an <u>ideal perfection</u>, forever on the wing, <u>presents itself</u> to the human mind. Continual changes are then every instant occurring under the observation of every man: the position of some is rendered worse; and he learns but too well, that no people and no individual, how enlightened soever they may be, can lay claim to infallibility;—the condition of others is improved; whence he infers that man is endowed with an indefinite faculty of improvement. <u>His reverses</u> <u>teach</u> him that <u>none</u> may hope to have discovered <u>absolute good</u>—his <u>success stimulates</u> him to the never-ending <u>pursuit of it</u>. [Thus, forever seeking—forever falling, to rise again—often disappointed, but not discouraged—he tends unceasingly towards that unmeasured greatness so indistinctly visible at the end of the long track which humanity has yet to tread.] It can hardly be believed how many facts naturally flow from the philosophical theory of the indefinite perfectibility of man, or how strong an influence it exercises even on men who, living entirely for the purposes of action and not of thought, seem to conform their actions to it, without knowing anything about it. I accost an <u>American sailor</u>, and I inquire <u>why</u> the <u>ships</u> of his country are built so as to <u>last</u> but for a <u>short time</u>; <u>he answers</u> without hesitation that the art of navigation is every day making such <u>rapid progress</u>, that the <u>finest vessel</u> would become almost <u>useless if it lasted</u> beyond a certain number of years. In these words, which fell accidentally and on a particular subject from a man of rude attainments, I recognize the general and systematic idea upon which a great people directs all its concerns.

Who crafted this absolute monster of a paragraph? My goodness. Wow. Well, let's see what we can do. One possible summary: perfection is attainable/stuff keeps improving? Sure, let's go with that.

Aristocratic nations are naturally too apt to narrow the scope of human perfectibility; democratic nations to expand it beyond compass.

One possible summary: Wait, isn't this already a summary? Oh well, let's craft our own. Human perfection is too narrow in aristocracy, too broad in democracy.

Okay kids, are you ready for the real party? This is the moment you've been waiting for. Let's kick that reading comprehension up a notch. Stand up; do a little stretch; listen to your game-day, pump-up tunes (just please, no *Jock Jams*. No one's riding that train.). All loose? Brain ready? *In-te-ger!* Too soon? Probably, but off we go!

Alexis de Tocqueville. *Democracy in America*. 1840.

"Chapter VIII: The Principle Of Equality Suggests To The Americans The Idea Of The Indefinite Perfectibility Of Man"
Just look at that beautifully descriptive title. You've overlooked it three times now, haven't you? Tsk tsk.

Equality suggests to the human mind several ideas which would not have originated from any other source, and it modifies almost all those previously entertained.

So, equality creates new ideas and modifies some older ones. Good enough.

I take as an example the idea of human perfectibility, because it is one of the principal notions that the intellect can conceive, and because it constitutes of itself a great philosophical theory, which is every instant to be traced by its consequences in the practice of human affairs.

Human perfectibility will be used to talk about equality because human perfectibility is both prominent and important.

Although man has many points of resemblance with the brute creation, one characteristic is peculiar to himself—he improves: they are incapable of improvement. Mankind could not fail to discover this difference from its earliest period.

What is a brute? Hmm... In the context, possibly an animal? Yes, that seems about right. So, humans can improve, animals cannot. Also, humans are able to observe this distinction. Otherwise, humans are similar to animals.

The idea of perfectibility is therefore as old as the world; equality did not give birth to it, although it has imparted to it a novel character.

What is this word "novel"? Curious. It seems rather important, too. Let's see. Perfectibility is old. Thus equality did not create it (give birth to it). But equality has... given it something. Well, if it's given it something, then it must be new. So let's assume that novel means new, generally speaking. Let's try this again: perfectibility has been around forever, but equality has added something new to it. That's probably close enough for us.

When the citizens of a community are classed according to their rank, their profession, or their birth, and when all men are constrained to follow the career which happens to open before them, everyone thinks that the utmost limits of human power are to be discerned in proximity to himself, and none seeks any longer to resist the inevitable law of his destiny.

So here's how we read this: "when citizens are classed according to rank yadda yadda yadda and constrained to follow the career... before them," everyone sees limitations based on their own lives. That's a bit depressing.

Not indeed that an aristocratic people absolutely contests man's faculty of self-improvement, but they do not hold it to be indefinite; amelioration they conceive, but not change: they imagine that the future condition of society may be better, but not essentially different; and whilst they admit that mankind has made vast strides in improvement, and may still have some to make, they assign to it beforehand certain impassable limits.

Now this is the mother of all sentences. Here-we-go, here-we-go, here-we-go, here-we-go. We've got this, kids. Let's look at this sentence's overall structure: "this, *but* that; this, *but* that; this, *but* that; *while* this and this¸ that." It's parallel throughout. Statement, then that statement's negation (or qualification)—four times in a row. Look at the sentence again. Do you see the three "buts" and the "whilst" (old-fashioned version of "while")? There's your structure. Now let's put that structure to use:

Not indeed that an aristocratic people absolutely contests man's faculty of self-improvement, but they do not hold it to be indefinite;

amelioration they conceive, but not change:

they imagine that the future condition of society may be better, but not essentially different;

and whilst they admit that mankind has made vast strides in improvement, and may still have some to make, they assign to it beforehand certain impassable limits.

Do you see the statement then counterstatement arrangement now? I'm going to present it in yet another way below. This time, I'm going to put all the statements together and all the counterstatements together, with each numbered for you so you can compare them:

Statements:

1a. Not indeed that an aristocratic people absolutely contests man's faculty of self-improvement

2a. amelioration they conceive

3a. they imagine that the future condition of society may be better

4a. and whilst they admit that mankind has made vast strides in improvement, and may still have some to make,

Counterstatements (Qualifying Statements):

1b. but they do not hold it to be indefinite

2b. but not change

3b. but not essentially different

4b. they assign to it beforehand certain impassable limits

That's the same selection of text, which I've tried separating for you in three different ways to highlight the structure of it. I realize I'm not physically there to talk you through it, but I'm hoping one of the ways I've presented it will help guide you through the text. Now let's try putting them all together.

Aristocratic people do not contest that people can improve (1a); they believe in amelioration (2a)—wait…what does that mean? Let's see if 3a and 4a help us out: future society *may be better* (3a); mankind has improved and can improve some more (4a). Boom! Amelioration must have something to do with improvement. Aw yeah, de Tocqueville can't handle your mad reading skills. It appears that the "a" statements address the idea that things can improve. Now let's look at the "b" side.

Improvement isn't indefinite (1b); complete, one-hundred-percent change doesn't happen (2b); society won't be essentially different (3b); there are defined limits on improvement (4b). So, basically, nothing has changed, even if marginal improvements can be made. That's certainly inspiring. Good pep talk.

Thus they do not presume that they have arrived at the supreme good or at absolute truth (what people or what man was ever wild enough to imagine it?) but they cherish a persuasion that they have pretty nearly reached that degree of greatness and knowledge which our imperfect nature admits of; and as nothing moves about them they are willing to fancy that everything is in its fit place. Then it is that the legislator affects to lay down eternal laws; that kings and nations will raise none but imperishable monuments; and that the present generation undertakes to spare generations to come the care of regulating their destinies.

Yadda yadda yadda—this is merely amplifying the prior sentence. Let's just move along.

In proportion as castes disappear and the classes of society approximate—as manners, customs, and laws vary, from the tumultuous intercourse of men—as new facts arise—as new truths are brought to light—as ancient opinions are dissipated, and others take their place—the image of an ideal perfection, forever on the wing, presents itself to the human mind.

Four lines for *one* sentence? Ye gods! Whatever, this is important, so we need to do this. Bear with me.

"In proportion" …now what could that mean. Well, let's see. In math, proportions always involve comparing different sets of numbers, or more simply, comparing things. In math, it would be 2 is to 3 as 4 is to 6, or something like that. Now that we have an idea of proportion (comparing things), let's keep moving.

"castes disappear"—hmm—like a system where you have a specific societal role assigned at birth? Okay, cool. And they're disappearing? Got it.

"and classes of society approximate"—what is it with these blasted math terms? This is supposed to be reading! Approximate, so like when we say 3.8 is approximately 4? But what does that mean in this context since there aren't any numbers? Let's see, 3.8 is close to 4, so does this mean as classes of society come close together? That seems like it could make sense here. Cool beans.

"as manners, customs, and laws vary, from the tumultuous intercourse of men—as new facts arise—as new truths are brought to light—as ancient opinions are dissipated, and others take their place"—so basically a bunch of new crap is happening. Just an FYI, dashes are usually used to amplify the statements before them and present a stronger interruption than commas. Anyway, all the stuff in the dashes basically seems to say "things are a-changin'."

"the image of an ideal perfection, forever on the wing, presents itself to the human mind."—so when people come close together and when new stuff is happening, *the idea of perfection seems real*. We've SO got this!

Continual changes are then every instant occurring under the observation of every man: the position of some is rendered worse; and he learns but too well, that no people and no individual, how enlightened soever they may be, can lay claim to infallibility;—the condition of others is improved; whence he infers that man is endowed with an indefinite faculty of improvement.

Ick. Let's hope the next sentence offers some clarity. I'll summarize this beast for us: changes reveal mistakes, but improvement remains possible.

His reverses teach him that none may hope to have discovered absolute good—his success stimulates him to the never-ending pursuit of it.

Here's the big question: what does "reverses" likely mean in the context of this sentence? Remember, we've already seen sentences where de Tocqueville showed us that he likes a parallel structure. If that's the case here, then "reverses" is the opposite of "success." So, it seems like reverses has something of the idea of "failures" or "setbacks" in the context of this sentence. To paraphrase this sentence: "setbacks show that no one's perfect, but success makes people think perfection is possible."

Thus, forever seeking—forever falling, to rise again—often disappointed, but not discouraged—he tends unceasingly towards that unmeasured greatness so indistinctly visible at the end of the long track which humanity has yet to tread.

I have to be honest. This is one of my favorite lines. This is probably because I run my own business. But I think it's important as well for those of you pursuing college, because there will be disappointments along the way. But you can't let them discourage you. Disappointments don't define you. Look at this sentence. "Forever seeking"—cool. Let's get after our dreams. "forever falling"—yeah, that's gonna happen when you dream big. "to rise again"—like the Phoenix, baby! "often disappointed"—yeah, failure is rough. "but not discouraged"—but I won't repeat those mistakes! "he tends unceasingly"—that's right, can't hold me down. "towards that unmeasured greatness"—I'll know what greatness is when I reach it. "so indistinctly visible"—it's there, but not quite crystalline. "at the end of the long track which humanity has to tread"—the road opens before us, indistinct, but full of opportunity. Are you inspired? Are you ready to screw up on your ACT and SAT prep? Are you ready to learn from those mistakes and "rise again"? Yeah you are. Wait, maybe Alexis de Tocqueville is a motivational speaker after all! Let's do this!

It can hardly be believed how many facts naturally flow from the philosophical theory of the indefinite perfectibility of man, or how strong an influence it exercises even on men who, living entirely for the purposes of action and not of thought, seem to conform their actions to it, without knowing anything about it.

Recapitulation of thesis, basically. Moving along.

I accost an American sailor, and I inquire why the ships of his country are built so as to last but for a short time; he answers without hesitation that the art of navigation is every day making such rapid progress, that the finest vessel would become almost useless if it lasted beyond a certain number of years. In these words, which fell accidentally and on a particular subject from a man of rude attainments, I recognize the general and systematic idea upon which a great people directs all its concerns.

YES!! A sailor. I know what a sailor is. This is great. When you're reading philosophy or works that are loosely philosophical in approach, like *Democracy in America*, grab on to any examples you recognize and hold on for dear life. You can start cooing lines from *Titanic*, "I'll never let go." You might want to keep those in your head, though, much like your "In-te-ger!" shouts.

So, we've got a sailor, and he says that ships don't need to last because we keep improving them. Basically, technology keeps on truckin'. We could also substitute a contemporary example for shipbuilding: who cares if your iPhone screen shatters easily? The screens don't need to last because a new, better phone will be released within the next year. Progress is endless! Aren't examples nice? I finally get what de Tocqueville has been trying to say about the idea of perfectibility in democratic nations—it's endless!

Aristocratic nations are naturally too apt to narrow the scope of human perfectibility; democratic nations to expand it beyond compass.

Hold on, is that parallelism I see? It is! Aristocratic society thinks too little of human perfectibility, democratic society thinks too much of human perfectibility.

Well, did you survive? That's actually a cool essay, isn't it? Once you think of iPhones, de Tocqueville's claims gain plausibility. Now, my treatment of this essay was fairly exhaustive. I mean, I analyzed it in two different ways, and I analyzed one sentence alone three different ways. That's borderline nuts. And it certainly won't work on a timed essay when you don't have the luxury of scrutinizing every inch of a text.

So why did I take you through such a detailed process? First, I know that if you can comprehend that essay, you can comprehend any passage you'll see on an SAT or ACT. Second, all of the tools that I modeled for you can be used when you are quickly moving through a standardized test, though you'll have to modify them to accommodate the time constraints of the test. Here are a few summative thoughts that might help:

Notice how little I actually underlined in each paragraph? I only underlined "operational" or "key" words. Not a single "the," and never more than four words underlined at a time—my underlining is minimalist. For a standardized test, minimal underlining helps your eyes process small bits. But only minimal underlining.

Underlining is what cognitive psychologists like to call a "low-utility tool." That's a fancy way of saying it doesn't help very much. That's why I'm always frustrated when I see poor students in AP classes who are taught to underline every stinking word on the page: it doesn't help you understand anything! You just "feel" like you're doing something, like you're learning. Well I don't want you to feel like you're learning, I want you to learn. All of that said, minimal underlining highlights enough key words that, when you're trying to scan a passage for specific information, a system of <u>limited underlining</u> will thrust important information before your eyes.

You have to go quickly through those passages. If you underline nothing, you have a blank page of text that you'll now get to scan a second time when you go to the questions. If you underline everything, or even just half the information, your eyes will be exhausted. What is important, and what isn't important? Worse, if you underline only half, you'll ignore the half you didn't underline. Do you really want to gamble that you've guessed correctly about which half to underline?

I should also mention that, if you think a whole sentence is worth noting or remembering, a great way to highlight that sentence without underlining the whole thing is to [set the important part off in brackets]. If you look at our first trip through de Tocqueville, I used brackets on two occasions.

Leaving underlining, and I could write an entire chapter on underlining, you'll notice that the essay probably made more sense the second time we tackled it. That's because we were analyzing it more through comprehensive summary than by individual bits. When you're doing everyday reading, it's helpful to summarize a paragraph in your head; when you're rushing through the ACT or SAT, it's helpful to summarize each paragraph with a quick note off to the side. If anything, this approach will help prevent your brain from becoming fatigued, which will in turn allow your brain to be fresh for those moments when you need to summon its every resource.

Let's summarize how you can use the tools I highlighted in this chapter on the SAT and ACT. A good rule of thumb is that four words per paragraph should be worth underlining. If you're underlining more than ten words in a paragraph, it had better be one big paragraph. Also, a quickly jotted, one-to-five-word summary of each paragraph will be of even more help than underlining. Combined, the two tools will help you master the SAT and ACT's reading sections.

Chapter 10: Private Training, Part 2

Now, let's give you a few passages to practice on. Our first one is again from Alexis de Tocqueville. I'm willing to bet you'll find this super easy to read after our work on his other chapter.

Alexis de Tocqueville. *Democracy in America*. 1840.

"Chapter XVIII: That Amongst The Americans All Honest Callings Are Honorable"

Amongst a democratic people, where there is no hereditary wealth, every man works to earn a living, or has worked, or is born of parents who have worked. The notion of labor is therefore presented to the mind on every side as the necessary, natural, and honest condition of human existence. Not only is labor not dishonorable amongst such a people, but it is held in honor: the prejudice is not against it, but in its favor. In the United States a wealthy man thinks that he owes it to public opinion to devote his leisure to some kind of industrial or commercial pursuit, or to public business. He would think himself in bad repute if he employed his life solely in living. It is for the purpose of escaping this obligation to work, that so many rich Americans come to Europe, where they find some scattered remains of aristocratic society, amongst which idleness is still held in honor.

Equality of conditions not only ennobles the notion of labor in men's estimation, but it raises the notion of labor as a source of profit. In aristocracies it is not exactly labor that is despised, but labor with a view to profit. Labor is honorific in itself, when it is undertaken at the sole bidding of ambition or of virtue. Yet in aristocratic society it constantly happens that he who works for honor is not insensible to the attractions of profit. But these two desires only intermingle in the innermost depths of his soul: he carefully hides from every eye the point at which they join; he would fain conceal it from himself. In aristocratic countries there are few public officers who do not affect to serve their country without interested motives. Their salary is an incident of which they think but little, and of which they always affect not to think at all. Thus the notion of profit is kept distinct from that of labor; however they may be united in point of fact, they are not thought of together.

In democratic communities these two notions are, on the contrary, always palpably united. As the desire of well-being is universal—as fortunes are slender or fluctuating—as everyone wants either to increase his own resources, or to provide fresh ones for his progeny, men clearly see that it is profit which, if not wholly, at least partially, leads them to work. Even those who are principally actuated by the love of fame are necessarily made familiar with the thought that they are not exclusively actuated by that motive; and they discover that the desire of getting a living is mingled in their minds with the desire of making life illustrious.

As soon as, on the one hand, labor is held by the whole community to be an honorable necessity of man's condition, and, on the other, as soon as labor is always ostensibly performed, wholly or in part, for the purpose of earning remuneration, the immense interval which separated different callings in aristocratic societies disappears. If all are not alike, all at least have one feature in common. No profession exists in which men do not work for money; and the remuneration which is common to them all gives them all an air of resemblance. This serves to explain the opinions which the Americans entertain with respect to different callings. In America no one is degraded because he works, for everyone about him works also; nor is anyone humiliated by the notion of receiving pay, for the President of the United States also works for pay. He is paid for commanding, other men for obeying orders. In the United States professions are more or less laborious, more or less profitable; but they are never either high or low: every honest calling is honorable.

Well, what did you think? Did this one make a bit more sense? Could you summarize it? Did you note the examples given? I'll go through the essay, and you can compare notes. I'll bet you were way closer to nailing this one on your first read than you were with Chapter VIII.

Alexis de Tocqueville. *Democracy in America*. 1840.

Chapter XVIII: That Amongst The Americans [All Honest Callings Are Honorable]

What the crap is an honest calling? Whatever it is, it's honorable. Maybe reading on will help.

Amongst a democratic people, where there is no hereditary wealth, [every man works to earn a living, or has worked, or is born of parents who have worked]. The notion of labor is therefore presented to the mind on every side as the [necessary, natural, and honest condition of human existence.] Not only is labor not dishonorable amongst such a people, but [it is held in honor]: the prejudice is not against it, but in its favor. In the United States a wealthy man thinks that he owes it to public opinion to devote his leisure to some kind of industrial or commercial pursuit, or to public business. He would think himself in bad repute if he employed his life solely in living. It is for the purpose of escaping this obligation to work, that so many rich Americans come to Europe, where they find some scattered remains of aristocratic society, amongst which idleness is still held in honor.

Hmm, I'm thinking an "honest calling" is a fancy way of saying "work/labor." Anyway, summary time: labor is normal and respected in America—even rich people are supposed to work. Also, fun fact: Americans run off to Europe if they want to be idle/lazy. (Note: this is according to de Tocqueville and in 1840, not present day...)

[Equality of conditions not only ennobles the notion of labor in men's estimation, but it raises the notion of labor as a source of profit.] In aristocracies it is not exactly labor that is despised, but labor with a view to profit. Labor is honorific in itself, when it is undertaken at the sole bidding of ambition or of virtue. Yet in aristocratic society it constantly happens that he who works for honor is not insensible to the attractions of profit. But these two desires only intermingle in the innermost depths of his soul: he carefully hides from every eye the point at which they join; he would fain conceal it from himself. In aristocratic countries there are few public officers who do not affect to serve their country without interested motives. Their salary is an incident of which they think but little, and of which they always affect not to think at all. Thus the [notion of profit is kept distinct from that of labor]; however they may be united in point of fact, they are not thought of together.

So... aristocratic societies don't like connecting labor and profit? Basically labor should only be for self-glory or virtue? Sure. Basically, people in aristocratic societies pretend they don't care about getting paid for labor.

[In democratic communities these two notions are, on the contrary, always palpably united.] As the desire of well-being is universal—as fortunes are slender or fluctuating—as everyone wants either to increase his own resources, or to provide fresh ones for his progeny, men clearly see that it is profit which, if not wholly, at least partially, leads them to work. Even those who are principally actuated by the love of fame are necessarily made familiar with the thought that they are not exclusively actuated by that motive; and they discover that the desire of getting a living is mingled in their minds with the desire of making life illustrious.

That first sentence clarifies both the preceding paragraph and this one. In democratic societies, labor and profit are connected. You work so you can get paid (increase your resources). Even people who "just want to be famous" still care about getting paid.

As soon as, on the one hand, labor is held by the whole community to be an honorable necessity of man's condition, and, on the other, as soon as labor is always ostensibly performed, wholly or in part, for the purpose of earning remuneration, the immense interval which separated different callings in aristocratic societies disappears. If all are not alike, all at least have one feature in common. No profession exists in which men do not work for money; and the remuneration which is common to them all gives them all an air of resemblance. This serves to explain the opinions which the Americans entertain with respect to different callings. [In America no one is degraded because he works], for everyone about him works also; nor is anyone humiliated by the notion of receiving pay, for the President of the United States also works for pay. He is paid for commanding, other men for obeying orders. In the United States professions are more or less laborious, more or less profitable; but they are never either high or low: [every honest calling is honorable].

Did you see the example? Did you coo "I'll never let go"? I'm guessing you didn't, but we had another easy-to-understand example: the President! And because the President gets paid, no one is ashamed to get paid. Also, those last five words are awesome. Every honest (i.e. not illegal or oppressive) calling is worthy of honor. That's a wicked cool idea. Not only is that the whole point of this essay, it's also an excellent way of thinking about people and their work.

Good? Mostly comfortable with that one? If you're still stymied, try having a history or English teacher guide you through it.

Time for a fun one. This author makes an argument that many others before him proffered, and it's an argument that is still widely supported by many writers and editors today, though not universally.

Sir Walter Raleigh. *Style*. 1897.

Let the truth be said outright: there are no synonyms, and the same statement can never be repeated in a changed form of words. Where the ignorance of one writer has introduced an unnecessary word into the language, to fill a place already occupied, the quicker apprehension of others will fasten upon it, drag it apart from its fellows, and find new work for it to do. Where a dull eye sees nothing but sameness, the trained faculty of observation will discern a hundred differences worthy of scrupulous expression. The old foresters had different names for a buck during each successive year of its life, distinguishing the fawn from the pricket, the pricket from the sore, and so forth, as its age increased. Thus it is also in that illimitable but not trackless forest of moral distinctions. Language halts far behind the truth of things, and only a drowsy perception can fail to devise a use for some new implement of description. Every strange word that makes its way into a language spins for itself a web of usage and circumstance, relating itself from whatsoever centre to fresh points in the circumference. No two words ever coincide throughout their whole extent. If sometimes good writers are found adding epithet to epithet for the same quality, and name to name for the same thing, it is because they despair of capturing their meaning at a venture, and so practise to get near it by a maze of approximations.

Isn't it nice to have an essay that isn't 600+ words? Let's see how we can navigate this.

Sir Walter Raleigh. *Style*. 1904.

Let the truth be said outright: <u>there are no synonyms</u>, and the same statement can never be repeated in a changed form of words. Where the ignorance of one writer has introduced an unnecessary word into the language, to fill a place already occupied, the quicker apprehension of others will fasten upon it, drag it apart from its fellows, and find new work for it to do. Where a dull eye sees nothing but sameness, the trained faculty of observation will discern a hundred differences worthy of scrupulous expression. The old foresters had different names for a buck during each successive year of its life, distinguishing the fawn from the pricket, the pricket from the sore, and so forth, as its age increased. Thus it is also in that illimitable but not trackless forest of moral distinctions. Language halts far behind the truth of things, and only a drowsy perception can fail to devise a use for some new implement of description. Every strange word that makes its way into a language spins for itself a web of usage and circumstance, relating itself from whatsoever centre to fresh points in the circumference. No two words ever coincide throughout their whole extent. If sometimes good writers are found adding epithet to epithet for the same quality, and name to name for the same thing, it is because they despair of capturing their meaning at a venture, and so practise to get near it by a maze of approximations.

First, this is from a book titled *Style,* so I'm guessing it has something to do with style. Judging from the first sentence, I'd say that it's specifically about writing style. I underlined the main part, "there are no synonyms," but I suppose we could add that good writers sometimes can't express themselves accurately and thus employ synonyms to attempt to give the general idea of what they mean.

Now for the last one. I'm actually giving you one of my essays that was published in *EdTech Digest* in 2013. This is written for educators and technologists, but I'm certain you're up to the challenge by now. I will not offer you any commentary after it, so you'll have to puzzle out its meaning on your own. If you're uncertain that you've grasped its main point or if you get lost in a side point, ask friends or teachers to help you.

Big Data and EdTech: a symbiotic relationship?

As someone who spends the bulk of his time analyzing standardized tests and standardized test performance, you might imagine that Big Data promises to be my biggest friend. I've found, though, that there is a tipping point where the data start to overwhelm any intelligible thought and, instead of providing instructive information, merely provide more information. As a relatively recent voyager in the educational technology world, I've had the luxury of working with hundreds of students, parents, and teachers while the EdTech world grew around me, with a large portion of my work spent analyzing data and describing the narrative it (or they) tell to those audiences. Now that I find myself a part of the EdTech world, I've noticed a recent trend in articles and in EdTech products: many, if not most, highlight the integration and the promise of Big Data. Which leads to a question about that integration, do Big Data and EdTech have a necessarily symbiotic relationship?

This question has importance for EdTech developers because it both determines *how* EdTech products get developed and *what* EdTech products get developed. Further, and this is the item of greatest import, if Big Data and EdTech are necessarily symbiotic in relationship, then the success of an EdTech venture designed with this assumption will be largely concluded successful if Big Data is still considered valuable. Or, to put it another way, EdTech's reputation and worth become tied to Big Data's.

While Big Data's precise definition is still in flux, we can comfortably assume that it involves data that has a torrent of "volume, velocity and variety." If that alliterative jargon seems like it needs explication, you'd be right. There are a number of longer definitions available from a quick Google search—I found 52.7 million responses in .33 seconds—but Big Data can be thought of as data amassed on a larger scale from a greater number of sources, often with real time or immediate response, than we're accustomed to having access. Or, we can think of it as being more than 52 million responses in less than half of a second.

Yes, Data is Important... But with Deliberation as Guide

Lest people accuse me of not caring about data, most of my present work is dependent upon it, and I entered this field knowing that. I like data and rely upon it for many aspects of my work. I have never found, though, that data replaced what my eyes were telling me (which, admittedly, could be considered a differently conceived repository of data), nor has data ever been presented to me without requiring some interpretive narrative to comprehend it. As I like to tell my ACT Science students, "Data without context is meaningless." And, as nineteenth century apothecary John Haslam noted, "Connection, to a great degree, is a contrivance of our own minds." These cautions ought to remain at the forefront of our consideration of data of any size.

Whether determined by the programmers' minds as they devise ways of sifting and presenting Big Data, or determined by the observers' minds as they advise others on the meaning of that presented Big Data, the question persists about whether all that data is really as connected or meaningful as we hope, without even addressing the question of what all this cataloguing means for us morally. If we place too much emphasis on this (not really) new tool, we run the same risk of error as some early 20th century philosophers with their high hopes for formal logic's promise.

Big Data and EdTech Design

Aside from the general caveats given above, the more immediate concern about the potential conflation of EdTech and Big Data (I don't think we've reached that point by any stretch) is that future educational technology tools would be limited to a design that can incorporate measurements of student performance. Or, EdTech tools that receive funding or press would exclusively be those that incorporate Big Data somehow, even if just in name but not useful function. These are not likely outcomes since videos for TED Talks and Khan Academy exist under the EdTech umbrella, broadly speaking. They are, however, possible scenarios and dispositions that those of us creating, cultivating, or utilizing EdTech tools in the classroom should be careful of fostering.

To return to the idea of EdTech and Big Data's intertwining in public and educational discourse, we want most of all to focus on the promise of EdTech specifically rather than on the promise of EdTech and Big Data jointly. This is not to ignore the vast potential that Big Data may possess, but rather to highlight that EdTech, generally speaking, is not merely another tool for learning, but an integral element in the contemporary classroom. If we conflate the two in our conversation, we run the risk of miscategorizing Big Data's function and allowing EdTech's growing promise to overshadow the concerns about Big Data that even senior statisticians at Google hold. EdTech and Big Data complement each other: they are not so integrally conceived that they demand each other's existence.

EdTech, The Dream Weaver

I'll conclude with the striking words of Margaret Sherwood (1864-1955) whose 1916 essay "The Other Side" has served as a helpful reminder to me not to place disproportional emphasis on the daily data—big and small—with which I am presented, and to consider how to include space for dreaming with the EdTech products that I employ with my students or help design for others' educational enrichment:

> "Take away from youth the power of seeing visions, of dreaming dreams, and you take away the future. It would behoove us to remember, perhaps, that the eras of great deeds have not been eras of analysis, but eras when the creative imagination was at work. Yet our modern mental habit is overwhelmingly a habit of analysis, for which science, in teaching us to pick the world to bits, is partly, though not wholly, responsible."

Chapter 11: An Outline of Success

In some ways, this entire book could have been reduced to just this chapter. Of course, then you'd have missed out on all the side training and other recommendations, which would have been a serious disservice to you. Still, this chapter offers the most initial utility.

Curiously, this was also the easiest chapter for me to write. That's mostly because crafting a ten-week plan of study leading into the SAT or ACT is super easy for me. While I tailor my program to each student, ten weeks is the most common window students are able to give me, and ten weeks is the minimum amount of time I will spend with most students before their first test. I'll do ACT first and SAT second. Feel free to ignore one if it doesn't apply to you. If you're still considering both tests, you can glance at each.

I should note that this plan is one intended for ten weeks during the school year. The other resources I've mentioned in this book can be used to supplement summer study or a different timetable.

After I've finished the ten-week plans of study, I'll include a ten-day-cram approach that you can apply to either test because I'm nice. I realize that not every reader will pick up this book with ten weeks to go. I don't recommend the ten-day cram, but I realize that for some of you it will be your only option. Good tutors can adjust to the realities that their students have. While I won't accommodate ridiculous requests from parents (e.g. improving a student's ACT score by 8 points in ten days[97]), I will occasionally take on desperate, last-minute cases with families who fully understand that I can't predict how much I'll be able to help. How much cramming helps depends on what happens to be holding a student back. For the vast majority of

---

[97] Can it be done? Yes. But not consistently and only when the student has a very specific set of issues, most of which require the most modest of mental adjustments, typically to recognize the reasoning model outlined in chapters 2 and 3.

people, last-minute cramming is insufficient for sizeable or even reasonable gains. Use the ten-week plan unless you are reading this literally ten days before your test. If you have five weeks or fewer, look at the ten-week plan and then modify it with the insights I've put in the ten-day cram.

Disclosure: I do incorporate *QuotEd Reading Comprehension* and *QuotEd ACT Science* into the program. I've incorporated them, simply enough, because I do rely upon those mobile apps with my own students. The apps make up a critical portion of my students' training, so if I'm truly revealing my approach to the test, then I have to include them in the study outline. You can certainly study without them, but I obviously wouldn't recommend it. There's a reason I wrote "critical" above. But enough of that, let's get into this. I should note that I'll start with some hyper-specific instructions and then let you modify the remaining suggestions to fit your individual schedule.

An Important Aside

Before I start this section, I need to address something. I waited for the ACT's new prep book, *The Official ACT Prep Guide, 2016-2017,* to come out because I intended to craft this chapter's recommendations precisely to the new book, even though I didn't need that book to write about the updates to the ACT. I waited, though, because I intended to use the new book with my students, and I knew my readers would want that information. But after looking the new book over, neither I nor any decent tutor out there will be using that book, or at least not that book alone, so I'm writing this chapter to give you access to how an industry insider might approach the test instead. If the ACT wants to publish a fetid, externally bloated book that has too few tests (including one that wouldn't qualify as "updated" by any reasonable person's standards[98]), the lamest "tips" you can find (and

---

[98] When your updated practice tests "Now with *Double Passages!!*" only have double passages in two of the three tests, and I'm expecting to purchase a book with double passages in every single one of the very limited supply of tests you've given me, that's misleading marketing. The full reading section in the third test of the fourth edition is already available in its entirety as the fourth test in the ACT's *third* edition,

that are also easily found on every generic test-prep advice column in existence),[99] and some horrific formatting (I haven't yet looked for printing errors in the tests themselves, but the "updated" third edition has a rather pivotal one), I guess that's the ACT's prerogative. It's mine to name its book a prodigious disappointment.

Truthfully, I almost didn't complete my book. The title makes me cringe with its pretense, however true it might be. I refused to complete it two years ago when it was an introduction away from

---

so it is not exactly updated nor inhabited by any double passages. If the ACT were a for-profit company, it might go bankrupt for putting out this sort of rubbish. Because it isn't (at least by government definition anyway), the poor kids who purchase the ACT's book and believe its marketing bull are at a severe disadvantage compared to the kids who pay for test prep. Congratulations, ACT, you've actually managed to tilt the scales and make test prep from even crappy test prep companies better than self-study or having teachers or volunteers help a student prepare. Now tell me more about your "incredible campaign" to honor those in education "doing more with less" because you "believe in college and career readiness for all." Or are the words "doing more with less" actually meant to describe those unfortunate souls who gullibly work with the ACT's new book?

[99] Here are two great examples just from the six tips the ACT gives for ACT Science. I'll paraphrase. The fourth tip: pay attention to the science terms used and what they mean. My reaction: "Oh, you mean reading words? Like what people are supposed to do and were planning to do on the test anyway, because words have meaning?" The fifth tip: use reason to select your answer. My reaction: "Oh, *now* I understand why you had the fourth tip, you don't understand the meaning of words (or how people function, apparently). You see, ACT, students *are* using reason to answer the questions. How else do you think they're answering the questions? Are you that dumb? They are even reasoning if they decide that they are better off guessing than trying. It might not be the reasoning you suggest, but even I have no idea what you mean to suggest when you encourage reasoning. I can't imagine how poor high school students must react to your recommendation to try using reason. Do you wish students to use a formal logic model, informal logic model, defeasible reasoning model, abductive reasoning model, or a combination of them? Your directions at the beginning of the ACT Science section imply a defeasible reasoning model, but I'm not certain you understand the very rules you've assigned to your pseudoscience section. Regardless, the difficulty for students is knowing what reasoning model(s) they ought to employ or what preexisting assumptions they have brought into the test which they should disband. Their difficulty isn't using reason. They are reasoning, and your hint hasn't helped them one whit to know how to reason better on your test."

being ready for publication because I was so repulsed by the whole premise of the book and principally its title. Because I wanted students to have access to the so-called hidden information that only the 1% see, I finally convinced myself that this book's value made it important to finish, and this was before I saw what a farcical example of a study guide the ACT had published. Even so, I've mostly hated knowing that I'll be known as "that guy."

After seeing the ACT's disgusting display of utter disregard for the people who will most rely on its book (no really, look at its doozy of a disclaimer on the copyright page), I am thankful I didn't give up on this project. While I may endure some well-deserved ribbing for being "that guy"—particularly from my friends—the teachers, students, schools, and parents[100] who benefit from this book are worth that ribbing. I may not have changed the conversation about the ACT (or SAT for that matter), but my goal is that students will at least have hope for improving their scores.[101] Though the ACT may have no interest in helping you, what follows is an outline of what an elite program looks like (the rest of my book adds whatever you need

---

[100] I wish I could add journalists to this list, but I don't have confidence that the media will actually write about the ACT's demonstrable disregard for underserved students. If we want to be polite, perhaps the ACT is just inconsiderate. A sin of omission, if you will. Perhaps, but lack of consideration for a population you claim to be concerned about seems, well, a curious paradox at best.

[101] You might wonder, "Why is he so passionate about this? I mean, doesn't he just work with 1% clients? Is this just guilt?" No, it isn't guilt. I don't feel guilt for receiving payment for providing my expertise. I do, however, care about those kids who are trying to self-study. And even more, I care about the volunteers, teachers, and students I help in workshops and training sessions. I know there are hundreds of thousands more people like them out there who I'll never meet and genuinely want to help students (wish to be helped, in the case of the students), but would be misled by the ACT's marketing into thinking they'll be helping (or helped) if they just use the ACT's new book. I've never quite believed the trope that standardized test prep creates inequality (I think it's symptomatic, but that the inequality highlighted by the presence of test prep would be there whether test prep is there or not. Namely, wealthy families have always provided for their children's education, test prep or no. Other college access portals like essays and grades can be bought just as easily as test prep and often are…), but the severe shortcomings of the ACT's new book has led me to question my own skepticism.

to flesh it out for your individual needs). Yeah, you'll have to put in a little extra time chasing down a couple of the resources I recommend, but you'll have access to resources that are often marketed to students for thousands of dollars. Consider your time invested in chasing those resources down as being paid out at $500 an hour. Let's do this.

Here's how we'll handle the ACT's tightfistedness with its tests in the fourth edition: we'll ignore it entirely for our preparations.[102] Order a cheap used copy of *The Real ACT Prep Guide, Third Edition* online or find a friend or neighbor with a gently used copy. Have someone erase all the filled-in answers from the book's previous user. Now, go get the practice ACT packet your guidance office has for you. It's also available to print off online. That gives you six ACTs you can practice from, one of which has a double passage in it (the practice ACT packet). If you need more practice tests and have time to use them before your first ACT, start pleading with students who have taken an ACT from the year before who might have ordered official copies of their test for their own review. Ask them if you can have that official copy now that they're done with it.[103] You can also bribe fellow classmates who might take an ACT earlier in the year than you to order a copy of their tests for both their and your review.[104]

---

[102] If you want to try the first two tests because they offer more double passages you can practice on, use a library copy, borrow a friend's used copy, or order the fourth edition if you have unlimited resources. The reading sections can also be practiced if you have a friend (probably a 2016 grad) who took either the April or June ACT in 2015 and ordered a copy of the test for review. Of course, you will have to convince your friend to relinquish his or her copy to you.

[103] For the record, neither you nor test-prep professionals can *copy* the tests because of copyright laws, but you can study from the one your friend ordered without any problems.

[104] Seriously, just tell them that you'll pay for the extra money it costs to order a copy of the test. Not every single ACT test date releases the test you've taken, but the December, April, and June tests have historically been released. So pester friends taking the ACT on those dates if you aren't. If you are the friend taking it on one of those dates, be a good friend and order a copy for your friends. Until the ACT releases a decent, actually-up-to-date prep book, you and your friends can help each other even the playing field with those who work with tutors like me.

Should you find that you need even *more* practice tests, the ACT releases a new official "Preparing for the ACT" PDF every few years that contains a free practice test. While those are hard to find on the ACT's website—if possible to find at all—they are readily available online to print off for free if you look, and you won't be breaking any copyright laws that I know of because the ACT has already publically published the test for everyone's free use.[105] If I've somehow missed some element of copyright law, go to your guidance office and see if they have old packets from years past. Should you be squeamish about printing something off from online, those packets that have already been printed are certainly yours to use.

I've now offered you several paths for finding good-enough, official materials to prepare with. I'm going to describe a plan of study as if you were using *The Real ACT, Third Edition* and the practice packet you can get from your guidance office or print off online.[106] You can adjust this plan to whichever materials you're using. Just swap one test in for another!

ACT Week 1

First order of business: review "Reasoning Part the First," "Reasoning Part the Second," and "Private Training"

Once that's over with, go through all the Reading passages in the first test in *The Real ACT, Third Edition*, applying the skills you've learned from this book. Do two passages your first day, and then do one passage a day over the next two days. All passages should be

---

[105] These old, freely-released practice tests are the ones I use with my students along with the ACT's official book.

[106] This is not to be confused with the free practice materials that are on the ACT's website. I strongly suggest using those before your *second* ACT, not your first. You do need some materials left over for future review. I prefer to use the website materials with my students before their second ACT because at this point they are annoyed with test prep, and the new training environment helps them to continue to improve.

done untimed and should be carefully corrected once you're through each passage[107]

Other bits for this week:

-Go to the Reading passages in the <u>fifth test</u> in *The Real ACT, Third Edition.* Do the first two passages on different days. Try the first passage in twelve minutes. If you can't complete it within twelve minutes, still finish it after time runs out. Most people (not everyone, though) can finish their first passage in about twelve minutes. For each passage after your first one, try cutting off fifteen seconds each until you're finally down to game-day pace (8:45 per passage)[108]

-Read the intro and first three chapters of *They Say, I Say*

-Read chapter 1 #'s 1-7 in the S&W

-Do five questions a day in *QuotEd Reading Comprehension*

ACT Week 2

-Go to the Reading passages in the <u>fifth test</u> in *The Real ACT, Third Edition.* Do the remaining two passages on different days

---

[107] An essential thing to note when you're correcting your work is which types of passages or questions you consistently struggle with. For example, passage III of the ACT Reading section is always a "humanities" reading passage. If you find that you're always missing five of the ten questions in passage III, but only two of the ten questions in passage IV (a "natural science" reading passage), then on test day you should skip passage III and do passage IV first. Always do your strongest passages first. I typically don't take stock of which passages a student is weak on until week 9 of study. Why? Well, you're learning to integrate a new mental approach to the test. The first few weeks can be a bit rough, but then you may suddenly turn a corner with particular passage types. So don't worry about types of passages or questions you struggle on, but do note them for later insight and review.

[108] If you're typically slower on standardized tests, you'll want to increase the number of QuotEd passages you use and drop the time limits a little bit more gradually. You may never get all the way down to game-day pace per subsection, but you can still reach a very good score if you aren't missing the ones you get to.

-Do two Reading passages from the <u>second test</u> in *The Real ACT, Third Edition,* on two different days

-Do the <u>first Math test</u> untimed (feel free to do over several days) in *The Real ACT, Third Edition*

-Read chapters four through seven in *They Say, I Say*

-Read chapter 1 #'s 8-11 and chapter 2 #'s 12-14 in S&W

-Do four questions a day in *QuotEd Reading Comprehension*

-Read through the "General Hints" and "Double Passages" in *QuotEd ACT Science*'s "Strategies" section

ACT Week 3

-Go to pages 198-199 in *The Real ACT, Third Edition.* Do the Science passage exactly as you've learned from this book's reasoning chapters, "General Hints," and "Double Passages"

-Do the Science passage on pages 480-481 in *The Real ACT, Third Edition*

-Do the remaining Reading passages from the <u>second test</u> in *The Real ACT, Third Edition,* on different days

-Do the first half of the <u>second Math test</u> with time[109] in *The Real ACT, Third Edition*

---

[109] If you're a math star, you should be able to complete the first thirty problems between 22 and 28 minutes with two misses or fewer. For this first practice round, give yourself 29 minutes. If you find that you struggle a bit more with math, your goal will be to finish the first thirty problems in 30-35 minutes with three misses or fewer. If you find math to be an alien, oppressive force (ACT Math scores below a 21), then you should aim for finishing the first thirty problems in 35-40 minutes with five to ten misses, and then you'll basically skip around the remaining thirty problems trying to find the five to fifteen problems that you recognize and/or are easy.

-Read chapters eight and nine in *They Say, I Say*

-Read chapter 2 #'s 15-22 in S&W

-Do four questions a day in *QuotEd Reading Comprehension*

-Read through "Graphs," "Tables," and "Diagrams" in *QuotEd ACT Science*'s "Strategies" section

-Do questions 1-10 in *QuotEd ACT Science*

ACT Week 4

-Go to the first Science passage in the <u>first test</u> in *The Real ACT, Third Edition*. Do it and then the two following it untimed, applying the strategies from *QuotEd ACT Science*. Then, try the remaining three passages in six minutes and fifteen seconds

-Do questions 11-40 in *QuotEd ACT Science*

-Do the ACT Science passages on pages 100-101, 105-106, and 110 on separate days in five minutes and forty-five seconds apiece

-Do one Reading passage from the <u>third test</u> in *The Real ACT, Third Edition*

-Do the second half of the <u>second Math test</u> with time[110] in *The Real ACT, Third Edition*

-Read chapters ten and eleven in *They Say, I Say*

-Read chapter 3 in S&W (a fast read with less importance for the ACT)

---

[110] For math stars, do it in 36 minutes; for middle-ground math peeps, do it in 38 minutes; for math avoiders, try it in 40 minutes. The goal is to learn how to work within the time. For later sections, cut down your time by one to five minutes if you can.

-Do four questions a day in *QuotEd Reading Comprehension*

ACT Week 5

-Do the entire English test from the <u>first test</u> in *The Real ACT, Third Edition*, untimed

-Do pages 42-48 in ten minutes per passage

-Do the ACT Science passages in the <u>second test</u> in *The Real ACT, Third Edition*. Try cutting down your time to five minutes and thirty seconds (game-day pace is five minutes flat)

-Do one Reading passage from the <u>third test</u> in *The Real ACT, Third Edition*

-Do the first half of the <u>third Math test</u> with time in *The Real ACT, Third Edition*

-Read chapter 5 in S&W (yes, skipping chapter 4)

-Do three questions a day in *QuotEd Reading Comprehension*

-Do one passage a day in *QuotEd ACT Science*

ACT Week 6

-Do the entire English test from the <u>second test</u> in *The Real ACT, Third Edition*, untimed

-Do the ACT Science passages in the <u>third test</u> in *The Real ACT, Third Edition*. Try cutting down your time to five minutes flat

-Do one Reading passage from the <u>third test</u> in *The Real ACT, Third Edition*

-Do the second half of the <u>third Math test</u> with time in *The Real ACT, Third Edition*

-Read chapters twelve and thirteen in *They Say, I Say*

-Review S&W chapter 1

-Do three questions a day in *QuotEd Reading Comprehension*

-Do one passage a day in *QuotEd ACT Science*

ACT Week 7

-Do the entire English test from the <u>third test</u> in *The Real ACT, Third Edition*, untimed

-Do the ACT Science passages in the <u>fourth test</u> in *The Real ACT, Third Edition*. Try cutting down your time to five minutes flat

-Do one Reading passage from the <u>third test</u> in *The Real ACT, Third Edition*

-Do two Reading passages from the <u>fourth test</u> in *The Real ACT, Third Edition* (do these together in 20 minutes or less)

-Do the <u>fourth Math test</u> (whole thing) in time in *The Real ACT, Third Edition*

-Read chapters fourteen and fifteen in *They Say, I Say*

-Review S&W chapter 2

-Do three questions a day in *QuotEd Reading Comprehension*

-Do one passage a day in *QuotEd ACT Science*

ACT Week 8

-Do the entire English test from the <u>fourth test</u> in *The Real ACT, Third Edition*, untimed

-Do the ACT Science passages in the <u>fifth test</u> in *The Real ACT, Third Edition*. Try cutting down your time to five minutes flat

-Do two Reading passages from the <u>fourth test</u> in *The Real ACT, Third Edition* (do these together in 19 minutes or less)

-Do the <u>fifth Math test</u> (whole thing) in time in *The Real ACT, Third Edition*

-Read chapters sixteen and seventeen in *They Say, I Say*

-Do five questions a day in *QuotEd Reading Comprehension*

-Do two passages a day in *QuotEd ACT Science*

-Review "Romancing Your Audience"

ACT Week 9

-Do the entire English test from the <u>fifth test</u> in *The Real ACT, Third Edition*, untimed

-Review chapter 8 in *They Say, I Say* and do Exercise 1

-Do five questions a day in *QuotEd Reading Comprehension*

-Do two passages a day in *QuotEd ACT Science*

-Do the whole practice test in the *Preparing for the ACT Test* packet you can get from school. Do this in one sitting with a scantron (tear one out from your red book). I recommend doing it at the end of the week on Saturday

ACT Week 10

The week before your test...[111]

---

[111] If you take the test on Sunday instead of Saturday or receive extended time and

Dear enterprising student,

Your doom is upon you. Too gloomy? Probably. Let's try again. Look, you've been preparing for nine weeks already, so you have to be in pretty good shape. You know what the test looks like; you know your strengths and weaknesses. Now it's time for you to place confidence in the work you've done. Trust the process. This first test is just a practice round. You've got all the skills in place, and it's simply time to try them out for realz yo. If any kinks are left, this test is the time to find them. Take this test as a glorified practice. Will your adrenaline be running? Heck yeah. Will you be more prepared than 99% of the kids taking the test? Absolutely. Go out there and find out what areas are still weak. You know what you're doing. Trust the work you've put in. Test day won't be perfect, but you've got technique and practice with it to guide you. Trust your technique; trust yourself.

Are you ready? Come on, let's have a little striking of that breastplate. "In-te-GER!!!!!" Let's do this!

Sunday through Wednesday the week before your test: Review *all* English and Math errors. Know them inside and out. You can also review any QuotEd questions that you like and anything in the S&W and *They Say, I Say* that you want. After Wednesday, there's *no more review of anything* in your books or apps. Why? Well, it's simply because the ACT is a comprehensive test and you'll need every ounce of mental plasticity in your body when you take the test. You've been reviewing for ten freaking weeks! If it isn't in your brain now, it will never be there. Get your math and English rules memorized over these four days.

Recently, I had a student who was absolutely freaking out the Thursday before his test. He begged and pleaded with me to let him review some of the math and English facts because he felt like they

---

are allowed to take the test over multiple days, please modify this to your needs. I've had hundreds of students for whom I've made this modification.

weren't steady enough. I told him to shut up and trust the process. Now that student's test a few months before had been a 33, and if we didn't get a 35 or 36 on this round, his parents would have been all over me for not producing the result they hoped for. So it wasn't like my own pulse should have been low. But I couldn't let that student undermine his work. He agreed to trust the process and didn't review after Wednesday. He scored a 36.

Every student who has decided that I must be an idiot and not know what I'm doing and then gone ahead and reviewed the two days before his or her test has underperformed by as many as 5 points on the ACT. You decide how dumb you want to be. I've warned you, but it's up to you to either trust your work or freak out and bomb the test.[112]

Thursday the week before your test: Take thirty minutes today to visualize the entire test, top-to-bottom. Think through the sections in order and envision precisely how you're going to dominate each one. Reflect on the review work you've done over the prior four days. When you're visualizing the English test, think through the concepts and missed questions you reviewed the prior four days. Then, visualize your performance on math. Did you read the questions thoroughly? What equations did you review? Keep them in your mind. Then, think through how you'll handle your ten-minute break—getting up and walking around and eating a quick snack. Up next, how did your practice Reading and Science tests go? How will you dominate those on test day? What adjustments will you make?

---

[112] Last-minute review *does help* people who haven't studied at all for the test and are simply reviewing ten days or a week before the test. That's because they are just learning the format of the test and the formulas or grammatical concepts which most frequently repeat. For those who have reviewed for a longer period than a week or ten days, hardcore study before the test screws them over because they are either overconfident because they've tested well just before or unconfident because they haven't tested well just before. Nothing good comes out of taking more sections the two days before the test if you've already been studying. This isn't a calculus test where there's a limited body of knowledge you need to bring to the table; the Reading and Science sections alone can pull from whatever random sort of topics they choose. You need your mental plasticity to survive.

How will you stay technical on those sections even if stuff is weird? Use your thirty minutes to map out every inch of the test in your mind—you will not open your books for this; it's all in your head!

Oh, and try going to bed tonight at the same time you intend to on Friday night. If you think 9:00 p.m. is a great time to hit the sack, see if it works for you tonight first…

Friday the week before your test: absolutely nothing related to standardized testing. I don't really care what you do other than *not* doing the following: partying the night before (this includes school dances), exerting yourself with the hardest workout of your week (workouts are great, but not ones that include the word "insane"), baking all day in the sun, or screaming on rollercoasters.

Saturday (game day): Get up, have breakfast, and dress presentably.[113] Pack two snacks. I typically suggest an apple and a brownie. The apple will fill you up and is nutritious, and the brownie is something that you should be able to eat even if you're a tad nauseated (plus, there's a minuscule caffeine pickup before the wretched Reading section). Once you're in the test, stay technical. Eat that snack and walk around on the break. And then take care of business after the break. You've got this. Stay technical.

Well that was fun. Let's head over to the SAT (or PSAT) side of things.[114]

---

[113] My rule is this: if you were to meet the president of the college which you wish to attend that you should not be ashamed of how you look. One caveat for the loophole brigade: no hooded sweatshirts from that school. The ACT is an interview; dress accordingly. I'm not suggesting that you should wear your itchiest sweater, but you should dress closer to regular business attire than startup wear. You can figure it out. If you go in your comfiest sweats looking like death warmed over, shockingly enough, you'll perform that way. You decide how many times you want to take the ACT…

[114] More practice tests are being released this summer for the SAT. I'd suggest using one of them as a pretest before you start studying. You can weave in the others as suits your study schedule.

SAT Week 1[115]

First order of business: review "Reasoning Part the First" and "Reasoning Part the Second"

Once that's over with, go through all the Reading passages in the first test in *The Official SAT Study Guide,* applying the skills you've learned from this book. Do two passages your first day, and then do one passage a day. All passages should be done untimed and should be carefully corrected once you're through each passage[116]

Other bits for this week:

-Study and work through pages 1-39 in *PWN the SAT*

-Read the intro and first three chapters of *They Say, I Say*

-Read chapter 1 #'s 1-7 in the S&W

-Do five questions a day in *QuotEd Reading Comprehension*[117]

SAT Week 2

-Go to the Reading passages in the <u>second test</u> in *The Official SAT*

---

[115] As a reminder, the "Performance-Enhancing Accelerators" chapter has additional books you can easily add to this study outline. That's why I've called it an outline. These are the core materials. Flesh it out with other materials that meet your additional specific needs.

[116] An essential thing to note when you're correcting your work is which types of passages or questions you consistently struggle with. Always do your strongest passages first. I typically don't take stock of which passages a student is weak on until week 9 of study. Why? Well, you're learning to integrate a new mental approach to the test. The first few weeks can be a bit rough, but then you may suddenly turn a corner with particular passage types. So don't worry about types of passages or questions you struggle on, but do note them for later insight and review.

[117] If the QuotEd SAT Math app happens to be around when you're prepping, plop it into your studies from the first week on!

Study Guide. Do two of them on two separate days in fifteen minutes per passage

-Study and work through pages 40-91 in *PWN the SAT*

-Read chapters four through seven in *They Say, I Say*

-Read chapter 1 #'s 8-11 and chapter 2 #'s 12-14 in S&W

-Do five questions a day in *QuotEd Reading Comprehension*

SAT Week 3

-Go to the Reading passages in the <u>second test</u> in *The Official SAT Study Guide.* Do two of them on two separate days in fourteen minutes per passage

-Study and work through pages 92-142 in *PWN the SAT*

-Read chapters eight through ten in *They Say, I Say*

-Read chapter 2 #'s 15-22 in S&W

-Do five questions a day in *QuotEd Reading Comprehension*

SAT Week 4

-Go to the Reading passages in the <u>second test</u> in *The Official SAT Study Guide.* Do the last passage in thirteen minutes

-Read chapters eleven through fifteen and the essay "Hidden Intellectualism" in *They Say, I Say*

-Read chapter 3 in S&W (a fast read with less importance for the SAT)

-Do five questions a day in *QuotEd Reading Comprehension*

SAT Week 5

-Go to the Reading passages in the <u>third test</u> in *The Official SAT Study Guide*. Do two passages together in twenty-six minutes

-Go to the Writing and Language Test in the <u>first test</u> in *The Official SAT Study Guide*. Do the whole test, untimed

-Go to Math Test – No Calculator in the <u>first test</u> in *The Official SAT Study Guide*. Do that whole section in time (twenty-five minutes)

-Study and work through pages 143-195 in *PWN the SAT*

-Read chapters sixteen and seventeen in *They Say, I Say*

-Study the first half of chapter 4 in S&W

-Do five questions a day in *QuotEd Reading Comprehension*

SAT Week 6

-Go to the Reading passages in the <u>third test</u> in *The Official SAT Study Guide*. Do two passages together in twenty-six minutes

-Go to the Writing and Language Test in the <u>second test</u> in *The Official SAT Study Guide*. Do the whole test in thirteen minutes per passage with each passage done on a different day

-Go to Math Test – Calculator in the <u>first test</u> in *The Official SAT Study Guide*. Do that whole section untimed

-Go to Math Test – No Calculator in the <u>second test</u> in *The Official SAT Study Guide*. Whole section in time

-Study and work through pages 196-246 in *PWN the SAT*

-Study the second half of chapter 4 in S&W and read chapter 5

-Do five questions a day in *QuotEd Reading Comprehension*

SAT Week 7

-Go to the Reading passages in the <u>third test</u> in *The Official SAT Study Guide*. Do one passage in thirteen minutes

-Review "Private Training" and "Pinpointing Your Folly"

-Go to the Writing and Language Test in the <u>third test</u> in *The Official SAT Study Guide*. Do the first two passages in eleven minutes per passage

-Go to Math Test – Calculator in the <u>second test</u> in *The Official SAT Study Guide*. Do that whole section in time

-Go to Math Test – No Calculator in the <u>third test</u> in *The Official SAT Study Guide*. Whole section in time

-Study and work through pages 247-301 in *PWN the SAT*

-Review chapter 1 in S&W

-Do five questions a day in *QuotEd Reading Comprehension*

SAT Week 8

-Go to the Reading passages in the <u>fourth test</u> in *The Official SAT Study Guide*. Do the first three passages in thirty-nine minutes. Do the remaining two passages in twenty-six minutes[118]

-Review "Romancing Your Audience"

---

[118] After you've taken the time to correct all of these, I'd look back over all four of your practice SAT Reading tests. Which sections did you struggle the most on? On test day, those are the ones to skip and do last (and really focus on if you have extra time at the end).

-Go to the Writing and Language Test in the <u>third test</u> in *The Official SAT Study Guide*. Do the remaining two passages in eleven minutes per passage

-Go to Math Test – Calculator in the <u>third test</u> in *The Official SAT Study Guide*. Do that whole section in time

-Go to Math Test – No Calculator in the <u>fourth test</u> in *The Official SAT Study Guide*. Whole section in time

-Review chapter 8 in *They Say, I Say* and do Exercise 1

-Review chapter 2 in S&W

-Do five questions a day in *QuotEd Reading Comprehension*

SAT Week 9

-Go to Math Test – Calculator in the <u>fourth test</u> in *The Official SAT Study Guide*. Do that whole section in time

-Do the full Writing and Language Test in the <u>fourth test</u> of *The Official SAT Study Guide*

-Do a full practice PSAT or recently-released SAT

-Review chapter 2 in S&W

-Do five questions a day in *QuotEd Reading Comprehension*

SAT Week 10

The week before your test…[119]

---

[119] If you take the test on Sunday instead of Saturday or receive extended time and are allowed to take the test over multiple days, please modify this to your needs. I've had hundreds of students for whom I've made this modification.

Dear enterprising student,

Mount Doom will soon erupt. A tad macabre? Probably. Let's try again. Look, you've been preparing for nine weeks already, so you have to be in pretty good shape. You know what the test looks like; you know your strengths and weaknesses. Now it's time for you to place confidence in the work you've done. Trust the process. This first test is just a practice round. You've got all the skills in place, and it's simply time to try them out. Take this test as a glorified practice. Will your adrenaline be running? Heck yeah. Will you be more prepared than 99% of the kids taking the test? Absolutely. Go out there and find out what areas are still weak. You know what you're doing. Trust the work you've put in. Test day won't be perfect, but you've got technique and practice with it to guide you. Trust your technique; trust yourself.

Are you ready? Come on, let's have a little striking of that breastplate. "In-te-GER!!!!!" Let's do this!

Sunday through Wednesday the week before your test: Review *all* Writing and Language and Math errors. Know them inside and out. You can also review any QuotEd questions that you like and anything in the S&W and *They Say, I Say* that you want. After Wednesday, there's *no more review of anything* in your books or apps. Why? Well, it's simply because the SAT is a comprehensive test and you'll need every ounce of mental plasticity in your body when you take the test. You've been reviewing for ten freaking weeks! If it isn't in your brain now, it will never be there. Get your math and grammar rules memorized over these four days.

Last fall, I had several students absolutely freaking out the Monday before their PSAT. They were paranoid that they couldn't possibly hit a National Merit Scholar qualifying score. They wanted a whole list of possible scenarios and questions from which they could review twenty-five hours a day.[120] Obviously, I wanted them to score high

---

[120] You think I'm exaggerating but both these students *and* their parents were nuts. I

enough to qualify for National Merit, but we had already prepared them so that they could score that high. Anything more wouldn't prepare them, but instead exhaust them and remove the very nervous energy you should want to have on test day. My students did settle down,[121] and they were all quite pleased with their PSAT scores.

Every student who has decided that I must be an idiot and not know what I'm doing and then gone ahead and reviewed the two days before his or her test has underperformed significantly on the SAT. You decide how dumb you want to be. I've warned you, but it's up to you to either trust your work or freak out and bomb the test.[122]

Thursday the week before your test: Take thirty minutes today to visualize the entire test, top-to-bottom. Think through the sections in order and envision precisely how you're going to dominate each one. Reflect on the review work you've done over the prior four days. What adjustments will you make? How will you stay technical on those sections even if stuff is weird? Use your thirty minutes to map out every inch of the test in your mind—you will not open your books for this; it's all in your head!

Oh, and try going to bed tonight at the same time you intend to on

---

had to tell them that I wouldn't teach them anymore if they wouldn't trust that I knew what I was talking about. Yes, I can and do fire clients if they get too ridiculous. There's a point where you can't help people, and I only take payment from people if I think I can still help.

[121] No word on whether any Valium was added to their parents' meals.

[122] Last-minute review *does help* people who haven't studied at all for the test and are simply reviewing ten days or a week before the test. That's because they are just learning the format of the test and the formulas or grammatical concepts which most frequently repeat. For those who have reviewed for a longer period than a week or ten days, hardcore study before the test screws them over because they are either overconfident because they've tested well just before or unconfident because they haven't tested well just before. Nothing good comes out of taking more sections the two days before the test if you've already been studying. This isn't a calculus test where there's a limited body of knowledge you need to bring to the table. You need your mental plasticity to survive.

Friday night. If you think 9:00 p.m. is a great time to hit the sack, see if it works for you tonight first...

Friday the week before your test: absolutely nothing related to standardized testing. I don't really care what you do other than *not* doing the following: partying the night before (this includes school dances), exerting yourself with the hardest workout of your week (workouts are great, but not ones that include the word "insane"), baking all day in the sun, or screaming on rollercoasters.

Saturday (game day): Get up, have breakfast, and dress presentably.[123] Pack two snacks. I typically suggest an apple and a brownie. The apple will fill you up and is nutritious, and the brownie is something that you should be able to eat even if you're a tad nauseated. Once you're in the test, stay technical. Eat that snack and walk around on the break. And then take care of business after the break. You've got this. Stay technical.

Okay, so that's the ten-week outline. If you have a longer period over which you can study, use more tests and materials. If you have more time within your ten weeks (you do), please add materials from "Performance-Enhancing Accelerators." On to the ten-day special.

Day 1: Take a practice SAT or ACT (whichever test you have in ten days).

Day 2: Correct and score your test. Find your weakness *and* figure out why you underperformed on sections you thought you were awesome at (if you did underperform on any). Understand how you missed

---

[123] My rule is this: if you were to meet the president of the college which you wish to attend that you should not be ashamed of how you look. One caveat for the loophole brigade: no hooded sweatshirts from that school. The SAT is an interview; dress accordingly. I'm not suggesting that you should wear your itchiest sweater, but you should dress closer to regular business attire than startup wear. You can figure it out. If you go in your comfiest sweats looking like death warmed over, shockingly enough, you'll perform that way. You decide how many times you want to take the SAT...

every problem the prior day. Read "Reason Part the First" and "Reason Part the Second." Do ten questions in *QuotEd Reading Comprehension*.

Day 3: Take an untimed section in your area(s) of weakness. Take a timed section in your area of strength. Correct everything and understand any misses (also read "Pinpointing Your Folly").

Day 4: Take a half-timed section in your area(s) of weakness (add one minute per passage or something) and correct it. Review any math or grammar concepts you've found were a little unsteady. Do ten questions in *QuotEd Reading Comprehension*.

Day 5: Take a timed section in an area of strength and correct it. Review all misses from your pretest and other practice tests in your area(s) of weakness. Make certain you still understand them. Read "Romancing Your Audience." Do ten questions in *QuotEd Reading Comprehension*.

Day 6: Take a fully-timed section in your area of weakness. Review all misses from your pretest and other practice tests in your area(s) of strength. Do ten questions in *QuotEd Reading Comprehension*.

Day 7: Take a fully-timed practice test. Correct and compare to Day 1's. What improved? What's still shaky?

Day 8: Review all old misses from all prior tests. Try noting similarities between missed questions. Take a timed practice section in any areas that still seem unsettled (*not* a full test though).

Day 9: Review all misses for about an hour. Think through how the test's structure affects you. Otherwise, enjoy the day.

Day 10: Test day! Make certain you have breakfast and pack two snacks. Good luck!

If you're using this book and you've got a question that this outline doesn't cover, feel free to shoot an email to info@knerrtutoring.com.

"In all your reading, hold to the conception of yourself as a thinker, not a sponge. Remember, you do not need to accept unqualifiedly everything you read. A worthy ideal for every student to follow is expressed in the motto carved on the wall of the great reading-room of the Harper Memorial Library at The University of Chicago: 'Read not to contradict, nor to believe, but to weigh and consider.'" Harry D. Kitson

Chapter 12: Applying Like a Boss

It's fairly simple. Test scores are only a minimum qualifier for colleges. They don't get you in. So if you're betting on your SAT or ACT scores (or AP scores) to get you in, you've been misled. I hate to be the one to disabuse you of the notion that a perfect score will get you into Harvard, but it's true.

So, how do you establish yourself as an absolute boss in your application? You establish yourself with your résumé, recommendations, and essays.

Now, at least half of my students work with private guidance counselors to help them pick universities and study programs. In those cases, I stay as far away from the application process as possible, but I'm not writing this book for those students. I'm writing it for you, and there's a decent chance that you don't have the advantage of a private counselor. Maybe you're like I was in high school and you believed the guff that the test-makers and universities sell.[124] Maybe you're too busy working a job, playing a sport, helping your grandparents, or attending a camp to visit a bunch of colleges and learn their preferences, at least as much as those are publically stated.[125] If that's the case, read on. If you have a

---

[124] I use "believed" here because if you still believe what the standardized tests say about themselves at this point in this book, then I've at least partially failed in my task. Little hint: if the universities have convinced themselves to accept the standardized tests ("test optional" schools still accept them for scholarships and to boost their website stats, so they aren't off the hook), then either they're quite stupid, playing the game just like the test-makers, or both. In many cases, my impression is both. You can make your own observations.

[125] In argumentation theory, unstated preferences are sometimes called "dark-side arguments," which, much like the dark side of the moon, are unseen. Unstated preferences have different names in psychology and rhetoric, but the important thing for you to know is that colleges have them. And just like people, educational institutions have unstated preferences they don't reveal to others and unstated preferences they don't know they even have. Your job is to snoop those unstated

private counselor, don't waste your time on this chapter—your counselor should already have told you these things in some fashion or another.

So with that said, let's get the résumé off the table first.

Speak to Me, Résumé

First, don't let your résumé be boring. Revisit *Microstyle* if you have questions. Second, use your résumé to highlight the things your essays and recommendations won't. Yes, the bits highlighted in essays and recommendations should be there, but your résumé is your individual opportunity to brag. If an activity bores you and everyone else, buttress it with a vivid description or remove it. The longest list doesn't generally win an admission officer's heart.

With your résumé, structure it so that the interesting activities that aren't referenced in your essays can pop out. This generally means listing them first, if you can. Have a family friend glance over the list. Ask them which activities stand out and which ones excite them. If it isn't the ones you want, try reworking your résumé. And then rework it again.

That should be enough for the résumé. Feel free to Google résumés or see if your guidance office has any samples. Teachers can help too. Just don't expect them to do the work for you. A polished résumé is fun to edit; a hastily-constructed résumé will generally encourage your teachers to apply the same care in editing it. If you give them your best work, though, they will likely give you the same in return.

---

preferences out as best you can and make certain you highlight the things that make you attractive to that particular university and hide the things that university would hate. Is this a tough assignment? Absolutely. Are you up to it? You've read the suggestions thus far and are reading this chapter, so I think you're up to it. You may also have your own private library by now thanks to my seemingly endless list of suggestions. Sorry!

Remember Why You Love Me

Ever have a friend say to you, "Why are we friends again?" If this has just been my experience, well, I find that hard to believe.[126] Even if you haven't had that experience, though, you can probably grasp my meaning. Such comments are usually said in jest (I think); but with your teachers, it might actually be the case that they don't know why you're friends.[127] Even if you're confident that you are your teachers' favorite, though, it's possible that the reasons you want them to write your recommendations are not the same as the things they'll write about you in their recommendations.

This doesn't mean your teachers are horrible people or that they don't remember you. What it means is that they are busy, and you may find it beneficial to help speed their writing process along. Now, I'm not suggesting that you tell your teachers what to write in your recommendation or how to write it, but I am saying that you should absolutely tell your teachers precisely what specific experiences you've had with them that led you to asking for their recommendation.[128] Not only does this suggest the things you'd like them to write about, but it also lets them know they're special to you. Yes, they're supposed to write about how you're special to them, but it certainly helps their goodwill if they think they've had some significant role in your life.[129]

Let me just note that recommendations are something earned over

---

[126] Of course, my willful disbelief could be further reason why people say this to me.

[127] In Aristotelian terms, that would probably be friends of utility. They teach you (and thus get paid); you learn from them (and thus don't begrudge them their salary).

[128] This can include that satirical limerick you wrote that the teacher raved about as genre altering, the after-school volunteer project you headed under a teacher's guidance, or even the class you struggled the most with but managed to survive with good grace.

[129] It doesn't exactly inspire you to write a great recommendation when a student is like "Hey, so I've got to submit a recommendation. You up for doing one?" This indifferent casualness might warm the hearts of a few teachers, but I don't think there's a crowd of such souls.

the course of your high school career. If you think a last-minute round of toadyism is going to land you a chorus of laudatory cheers from your teachers, well, you might deserve the recommendations you receive. Providing you haven't left yourself in need of the Toady Express, it's best to ask your teachers for recommendations in the spring of your junior year.[130] That way, they have time to write them and you're first in line for completed recommendations, which means you can submit your college applications on time for any deadlines.

Recommendations are wild cards. For most students, recommendations are the differentiating factor. Almost everyone has the right grades and test scores. Most of those folks will have equally distinguishing essays. Recommendations separate the masses. "Such and such is a nice person" will not win you entrance to most colleges and universities if the rest of your application is at or below average. Choose people who can write a recommendation that will highlight a particular quirk or sensational skill that the rest of your application simply cannot address. Your essays can only communicate so much of you. Recommendations are your best chance to round yourself out as a three-dimensional human being in your application.

So You'd Be a Flying Squirrel...?

Tell me more. You've got to love the essay prompts you're given. Sometimes I think it would be easiest to just throw up your hands at

---

[130] This reminds me, though, of another bit about reputations being earned over the course of your high school career. If you are a beady-eyed, little grade-obsessed ogre (do you note my tone of disgust?), your recommendation will likely reflect that character flaw. Related: if your semester is complete (particularly the one spring of your junior year), don't email all of your teachers asking if they can suddenly nudge your grades up a tad. First, you're being completely inconsiderate of their time because they now have to email you instead of doing all the grading they'd like to get done so that they can be on summer break like you. Now you look like an ogre *and* an inconsiderate donkey. Nice work there, sparky. Second, you had a whole semester to nudge up that grade. Figure it out sooner and your recommendations will instead be the beneficiaries of the nudge you're trying to gain on your grades. Better grades and better recommendations. Would you look at that.

them and send the admission's office a picture of a chair with the word "empty" written above it in lieu of the essays. One school out there might like it, but the rest would all hate it, so we're probably stuck writing those essays.

There are really only two books you'll need to help you write a fantastic essay. There are a bunch of "Write Your Application Essay in 5 Minutes!" books out there, but I have yet to read an exciting essay drawn from one of their prompts. Remember, no one wants to be bored. Please don't become a bore.[131] *How to Win Friends and Influence People* by Dale Carnegie and *Bird by Bird* by Anne Lamott will help keep your writing interesting. Wait, are you done laughing at the first book's title yet? Come on, let it out. Done yet? No? Okay, 5 more seconds. Now let's get into why these books rock.

I was first forced (yes, forced) to read *How to Win Friends and Influence People* as a senior in high school, after I'd already written my college application essays. Fortunately, I read it before I had my college entrance interviews, and that definitely saved my bacon in one interview. Let's just say it wasn't going so well. I only salvaged a near-disaster by finding that we both collected things, him matchbooks and me spinning tops (wait, is this book's title an intentional rather than accidental double entendre?).

Unlike me, you have the opportunity to dive into Dale Carnegie's charm before you write your essays. Do you remember the chapter on romancing your audience? Well, what do you think your

---

[131] At this point you're probably thinking, "Like you?" Yeah, like me. I'm too old to be cool. I know. This doesn't bother me. Just remember old people don't like being bored. We may not be cool, but it's actually easier to bore us than it is you. True boredom is reading a tedious essay that either tries too hard to impress you or presents precisely the opposite problem—no effort is made to edit or think about whether your essay has communicated anything to anyone other than yourself. I know you were probably taught that your writing should be an extension of you, and that's true in a way. It should be an extension of you that communicates you or your ideas to another person. If your writing's just verbal tone poem to yourself, where the music is heard only in your ears, you might find difficulty in convincing others of your genius or promise. There are exceptions of course, but...

application essays should focus on? If you don't like your reader, or don't even think about your reader, your essays will likely exhibit that in some way. But if you're constantly thinking about your audience, wondering what they might think of this word, or this line, then your essay has a chance to excite them. It has a chance of helping them like you. It might even make them want to have coffee with you.

Dale Carnegie writes like a regular person, which is an important style to keep in mind when you're writing your application essays. Very few people wish to associate with pretentious people, and the only thing worse than a pretentious person is a person who is trying to act pretentiously but failing. Please, spare us your pretense and give us a sense of your interests and aspirations, even if they seem mundane. If you value something enough to invest time on it, you can make your reader appreciate why you value it so.

But Carnegie's style isn't the primary reason you should read him; the primary reason is Carnegie's steady encouragement to think about others in your everyday interactions. If you're constantly thinking about your reader as you write, your story will flow better. Further, you will revise your writing until it represents you and resonates with whoever might read it. While it appears a simple thing to think about your audience, appearances are certainly deceiving. Even accomplished writers occasionally struggle to connect with their audience.[132]

Of course, you'll benefit in other ways from *How to Win Friends and Influence People*.[133] I've read scores of books on dispute resolution, negotiation, mediation, and argumentation theory.[134] It's a weird

---

[132] For what it's worth, I don't consider myself an accomplished writer, but I do hope that I've connected well enough with you in this book that you will know how to approach your next standardized test.

[133] For even more, see "Appendix B."

[134] I also took a graduate course in alternative dispute resolution at *Marquette University*. Then I found the bookshelf that had the books from all the other courses in that graduate program. A few library fines and book shipments later, I'd learned

hobby, yes, but it actually overlaps with my research on standardized testing. Here's the thing: I've yet to read a book that covers those topics better. Oh, I've read books with awesome case studies, and I've read books that cover specific elements of those fields. I have yet to find a book that covers the overall material in a more accessible way. So, when you're reading the book, you'll find yourself learning negotiation tactics and interview skills: two things generally not taught in college and two things you'll definitely need if you work or rent an apartment while you're in college.

Turning to *Bird by Bird*, have you ever thought about what genre college application essays fall in? Your essays are really just memoirs. Fragmented bits of your life. Now, how often have you been asked to write a memoir in school? In fact, how many people write memoirs before they turn forty? The whole exercise seems impossible.

So let's make it less painful. *Bird by Bird* is a memoir. A memoir by a professional writer. A writer memoiring about writing. (That's right, for the fastidious grammar police, I just verbed a noun. Twice.) Anne Lamott will take you by the hand and guide you through the terrors of memoir writing. Along the way, her memoir's reflections will coax out reminiscences of your own life.

When you're reminiscing, jot those memories down. Keep collecting them as they spring into your mind. It's far easier to cut out memories than it is to add them in when you can't think of what else to write. Worry about how to integrate those memories later.

The weaving of memories into a coherent narrative, even one with seemingly disparate parts, is where Lamott's writing will help you the most. As you read about her life as a writer, you'll experience her vignettes of struggle, heartache, encouragement, elation. Each vignette will help you learn to weave your own.

Sadly, I did not read *Bird by Bird* until after college. I wish that I'd

---

what I wanted for thousands less than the full master's degree would have cost me.

read it before I had to write my own application essays. When I work with my students on their own essays, I sometimes cringe when I think about how poorly my own would look in comparison to theirs. Fortunately, my students will not experience that same disgust, in part because they've learned how to write memoirs.[135]

So those are my two book suggestions for awesome essay writing. Other books could be added to the list, some of which I've already mentioned. The most important thing is to write a rough draft. Then ignore it for a few days. Then rewrite it. Then revise the rewrite. Analyze your microstyle (individual sentences) and your macrostyle (full paragraphs and the full essay). Make certain they work together. Then, as Dale Carnegie advises, think of what your audience wants to know. And if you haven't told them, revise your essay until it's told. Word by word.

---

[135] My favorite memory is of a student who wrote about swimming for his application. The prompt was something along the lines of "Where do you feel most at home?" This kid *lived* in the water, both as a competitive swimmer and as a lakeside dweller. I asked him to write down a bunch of thoughts immediately after the next time he swam and then to write down several more thoughts the following day, but without looking at the prior day's thoughts. Then I started having him work those thoughts into his essay. Not once did I organize his essay or write his experience for him. I constantly pointed out places where the ideas didn't connect and kept making him revise and revise again until that essay shone, never once letting my writing style or ideas interfere with his essay. When we finished, he had an essay that could only have been written by him, but it was definitely the best version of him. Aside from remembering his essay (because it was awesome and 100% him—I seriously wish I could have written it), I remember most what he thanked me for when we were through writing it. He said, "You taught me how to write. This is the first time I didn't just throw words down on a page and think that was good to go. You made me think about who was reading it. I get writing now." He got into his top-choice school, one he didn't think he had a chance at. (No, it wasn't an Ivy. Not everyone dreams of Ivy League schools.) His insight should be your insight. Think about your reader. Revise your application essays until only you could have written them for that reader.

"Good writing is not dependent upon long or ornate or unusual words; it is the outcome of a constant use of the right word—the word that best conveys the author's idea." Flora Klickmann.

"Real novelty of vocabulary is impossible; in the matter of language we lead a parasitical existence, and are always quoting."
Sir Walter Raleigh. *Style.* 1904

"If you would be pungent, be brief; for it is with words as with sunbeams—the more they are condensed the deeper they burn." Robert Southey.

Appendix A: Repeat Offenders

I shoved the repeat offenders section in an appendix because I had no interest in including it in the main body of text. Most of this information can be discovered quite easily as you go through your own studies. Much of the rest can be found in the supplementary materials I've recommended.

I've included this section for two reasons. First, some Amazon reviewer would likely find it necessary to skewer my book for not including the things I've never advertised my book would include, so I add them here in an attempt to stave off moronic reviewers.[136] Second, I realize that you might not immediately recognize these as some of the most commonly asked concepts, simply because you have to focus on so many other things as you prepare. I trust that this section, then, will be worth including in such undignified lands as appendices seem.

I'm covering English[137] and math here only. This book has overwhelmingly focused on reading and reasoning, so I don't think you need more reading work here. As for science, most questions can be easily addressed through practice and by using *QuotEd ACT Science*. There is literally nothing I can think of adding here on science or reading that would offer anything other than repetition and boredom.

---

[136] I realize this is a futile task and that I will likely have such a review anyway because some schmuck will read the first chapter of my book, look at the table of contents, and decide to give me a scathing review without actually having read my book. Fortunately, I'm not trying to help that schmuck but the rest of you who have taken the time to try learning from my book. That said, if you find something unaddressed that you'd hoped to see, please contact me or include that in your review. If I write a second edition, I will certainly take your thoughts into consideration. I also have a section on my website where I can answer some of those questions which might come up.

[137] English for both ACT and SAT. Just because the SAT gives it a different name doesn't make it much different. The two tests' English sections are only slightly more different than the difference presented by naming something catsup or ketchup.

For the English section, I strongly suggest that you make yourself a little English reminder card, even if you have everything down from the books I've recommended. You want to be a paranoid little mole person who only cares about every jot and tittle of the English language, particularly of the prescriptivist sect. Is that insane? Yes. So is not improving your score on the one section of the ACT and SAT that you will likely have enough time to finish. I give you the card below:

<u>English Card:</u>

-Be Consistent with Your Usage

    a. Subject-verb agreement
    b. Noun-pronoun agreement
    c. Parallel structure[138]
    d. Verbs[139]
    e. Prepositional phrases[140]
    f. Adverbs[141]

-Be Concise[142]

-Be Active

    a. Avoid passive verbs, being, and "-ing" verbs in general[143]

---

[138] In S&W, this is in the subsection headed by "Express coordinate ideas in similar form."

[139] If you see a verb underlined, ask yourself two questions. First, does the tense match the rest of the sentence or paragraph? Second, does the subject match the verb? Yes, the second question deals with subject-verb agreement.

[140] Namely that they are adjectives that come after the noun they modify and should be *ignored* for most questions.

[141] The big insight here is that they *must* end in "-ly." Also, they can modify other adverbs, adjectives, or verbs, but *not* nouns. Keep that in mind.

[142] This is literally your flagship rule. Shortest wins in case of a tie. If you're at all in doubt, always choose the *shortest* answer. This includes punctuation like commas. Commas make things longer, too. With that said, note that I said "in case of a tie" and "in doubt." Don't use this flagship rule in place of your brain. The rule is there to help you when you're stuck, not to allow you to test on autopilot.

-Be Aware of Context[144]

-Be Confident—trust your instincts

There's your card. Now let's look at one commonly-tested punctuation question. I explore it mostly so that I can footnote my favorite dig which I share with all of my students. Grammar pedants, shield your eyes and look away.

If I were to ask you to name the founder and CEO of Facebook, I trust that you might name Mark Zuckerberg without much hesitation. In fact, I've already "named" the person who is Mark Zuckerberg with the phrase "the founder and CEO of Facebook." There isn't any other person you'd imagine in the world. This naming of things is quite important for the ACT and SAT.[145]

Here's why: for either test, the simple rule is that you must have either *two* commas or *zero* commas between your subject and verb. What you can never ever ever ever ever ever ever ever ever ever ever have is a single comma between your subject and verb.[146]

---

[143] I wrote *avoid*, not never ever choose. Though in the case of "being," never ever choose it on the ACT. And yes, I did use an "a" without having a "b" after it in a list. You know why I used an "a" instead of an asterisk? When I was in high school, I had it beaten into my head that an "a" always had to be followed by a "b," as if the "a" were somehow causative of the "b" or causative of a list itself. But an "a" to my mind is merely a symbol, and a symbol can be used in a list or as a separate marker. I have yet to be persuaded otherwise, and I thus gleefully invite you into my apparent corruption of the English language.

[144] Yeah, I may look like Captain Obvious, but you'll be the one suffering if you ignore this directive. Look around once in a while, why dontcha. Supposedly smart kids can't seem to get enough of only looking at the part of the test that's underlined. Please don't help the test-makers in their mission to screw you over.

[145] In the S&W, it's covered in chapter one, subsection three, under the discussion about restrictive and nonrestrictive clauses. In other resources, it's often discussed in terms of essential and nonessential clauses.

[146] By the way, for the clowns that think you're illiterate if you put a single comma between a subject and verb, I refer you to the seventeenth, eighteenth, nineteenth, and even early twentieth centuries. It's only recently that the preference for double or zero commas has become quite so forcible in its hold over most published writing.

Back to naming, watch what happens when I write the following:

The founder and CEO of Facebook, Mark Zuckerberg, is a new father.

Mark Zuckerberg is a new father.

The founder and CEO of Facebook is a new father.

Now why would I place commas around Mark Zuckerberg in that first sentence? Well, if I remove Mark Zuckerberg from the first sentence, do you have any difficulty thinking of the fellow running the world's biggest social network? I doubt it. To put it another way, cover up the first two sentences and look at the last one only. Is it difficult to think of the person I'm talking about?

The reason I put commas around Mark Zuckerberg in that first sentence is that I've already "named" him before I even write his name. There is literally no other person on earth who could be the founder and CEO of Facebook. So I put commas around Mark Zuckerberg's name in that first sentence because you can get my meaning without it there. It is basically extra information. Nice information, mind you, but extra. I don't need it to figure out who is a new father. It's the founder and CEO of Facebook.

If, however, I write, "My friend Greg is a new father," I can't put

---

For the ACT and SAT, you *cannot* use a single comma between a subject and verb. Keep that in mind. For the rest of your writing, realize that many people will object and some publishers will not let your writing see the light of day with the single comma between a subject and verb. With all of that said, if you want to use one because you think your sentence needs that brief pause of reflection upon your first idea before your verb bends it in service of the ideas that follow, then use your comma and glare with haughty disdain upon those who complain and are too uneducated themselves to know that their comma preferences are mere modern affections. Grammar pedants are the best to mess with. As a reminder, the ACT and SAT aren't messed with because you're filling out a scantron. Rock their stupid tests, and then you can spend the rest of your life writing to communicate instead of answering to their exacting standards.

commas around his name. Eh? You see, if I write only, "My friend is a new father," you might think I'm talking about my friend Nathaniel or any one of my many other friends who have recently become parents. "My friend" does not *name* a specific individual,[147] even if it describes how I feel about certain individuals, so I must have Greg's name included in my sentence for my meaning to have any chance of conveyance to you.[148]

Let's try two more examples, side-by-side. The first will already have "named" the person before we actually get to that person's name and thus will have two commas setting off that person's actual name from the rest of the sentence. The second will have not have "named" the person by the time we get to that person's name.

> My youngest nephew, Alexander Imhotep the Eighteenth, has a thing for pyramids.[149]

> The idiot who decided to write this book would rather be eating dinner now.[150]

Before I get my dinner, however, I suppose I should give you the math formulas you will find helpful for your test day.

I want you to make notecards with titles for these formulas. I didn't include the formulas themselves because I want you to look them up and write them down. I also want you looking them up so that you

---

[147] Okay, fine, smart aleck. If I only had one friend in the whole wide world, then writing "my friend" would indeed name that person. I have more than one friend. This is as much a surprise to me as I'm sure it is to you.

[148] To make matters worse, I have multiple friends with the first name of Greg, so unless context gave away which Greg is a new father, I'd have to write Greg's last name as well in order to make my meaning clearer. You can figure out how the specificity game can get increasingly difficult should the Greg I intend to name have a last name like "Smith."

[149] Names may have been changed to protect the innocent.

[150] If I decide to remove "who decided to write this book," you might think I intended to talk about one of the people who created the ACT's substandard prep book or even Dostoyevsky's Prince Myshkin.

can learn how to use them should you not remember.[151]

First notecard: <u>Measuring Triangles (aka Trigonometry)</u>[152]

Area of triangle

Pythagorean Theorem

Sine, cosine, and tangent[153]

Second notecard: <u>Circles</u>

Circumference

---

[151] I also didn't write them all here because they'll likely appear in that math app I mentioned...

[152] This card will make up roughly 15% of your ACT math score and a decent chunk of your SAT math score.

[153] Fun story about this trio (no, not SOHCAHTOA, but you should look that junk up). You see sine, cosine, and tangent each have a buddy. Those buddies' names are secant, cosecant, and cotangent. Now, you don't need to memorize how the buddies work *if* you can remember two simple things (well, maybe three). **First**, each partnership is formed by one of the two buddies having the prefix "co-" in its name. You may recognize that prefix if you have coworkers (people with whom you work), if you cohabit (live with) a legal guardian, or if you've ever met someone who was a co-owner of a business. The prefix "co-" simply means "together" or "with." **Second**, if you can figure out who cotangent's buddy is, you can pretty easily figure out how the rest pair off. This is indeed as simple as it seems. Cotangent pairs up with tangent. Now we have to figure out how sine and cosine would pair off with secant and cosecant. Fortunately for us, we have that first simple thing to keep in mind: each partnership has to have *one* buddy with the prefix "co-" in it. So sine has to pair with cosecant and cosine has to pair with secant (because cosine already has a "co-" in it). Thus, our pairs are sine-cosecant, cosine-secant, tangent-cotangent (or in math shorthand: sin-csc, cos-sec, tan-cot). **Third**, take the buddy from the original trio and flip it upside down to find its pal. So if sine happens to be 6/7, then cosecant (sine's pal) is 7/6. The buddy system is great. Read this through a few times if I went too fast. I realize this isn't how they explain it in math class. If you can remember it from math class, why'd you waste your time reading all this?

Area

Volume of a sphere[154]

Volume of a cylinder

Equation of a circle[155]

Third notecard: <u>Lines</u>

Equation of a line (in slope-intercept form)

Slope of a line

Midpoint formula[156]

Distance formula[157]

Fourth notecard: <u>Random Formulas</u>

This is the card for formulas that you see appear on more than one

---

[154] This one is typically given to you on the ACT at least, but you should still be comfortable with it.

[155] The ACT *loves* this one, and students never seem to know it. The SAT has questions related to it, too.

[156] Hint for those who can't remember this one. If it's a *mid*point, then it's halfway, yes? And if something is halfway, isn't it just the average? I mean, halfway between six and ten is eight, which is the same as the average of six and ten. If you can't remember the equation, average your two x values and then average your two y values. Also, make certain they didn't give you the midpoint and ask you for an endpoint instead. As noted throughout this book, read the question.

[157] Yeah, super-sleuths can figure this out with the Pythagorean Theorem alone (from which the distance formula is derived). If what I said just now makes zero sense to you, this isn't your shining moment as a super-sleuth and you should go ahead and memorize the handy-dandy distance formula which appears on almost every ACT and appears on occasion on the SAT.

test but that you can't seem to remember. Perimeter, area (particularly of a trapezoid[158]), volume, summation of a series—whatever stands out to you as a formula that you've seen at least twice but keep forgetting.

---

[158] The area of any four-sided object is base times height, right? But with a trapezoid, you have *two* bases, not one. Here's what you need to remember about trapezoids. First, height is always based on the *right angle* height, not the slant height of the sides of the trapezoid. Second, if you have two bases, you just have to average them so that you can easily plug the result into your base times height formula. To repeat, average the two bases in the trapezoid and multiply by the height to find its area. This is mostly an ACT concern as of this book's publication.

Appendix B: Eager Beavers (Prepping Before Junior Year)

Sometimes people ask me when they should start prepping for the ACT or SAT, specifically if they can start prepping *before* they are high school juniors or seniors. There are actually two answers to that question. The first is that only a charlatan or imbecile would do straight test prep sooner than the summer leading into a student's junior year.[159] Amusingly, I know of one high school in my area that teaches a hybrid ACT prep and speech class to its sophomores. For as many times as I hear people railing against those in the test prep community as leeches on the educational soul of the world,[160] it entertains me greatly that a school would invest time and resources to offer a course that is considered bad practice by just about any expert in the test prep world. Frankly, if that course focused on a rigorous exploration of elocution and oratory, the students would be far more prepared for life and the ACT.

This leads me to my second answer: test prep which isn't ACT- or SAT-specific can be beneficial to a student prior to the summer leading into junior year. Now, I'm not talking about generic study, since there should be some view towards the tests, but preparation at this stage should be all about training for the tests, not replication or practice test

---

[159] A number of excellent tutors made exception to this rule when the SAT was transitioning to its "new" form. Because many students wished to take the old SAT in the fall of 2015, and those students had a limited window in which to prepare, tutors made exception to accommodate the shortened timetable for preparation. Sometimes unfortunate circumstances call for flexibility, but "trying to get a jump on things" isn't an unfortunate circumstance, lest there is some confusion for any overzealous readers of this book.

[160] If you think I'm being dramatic, that's actually a diplomatic way of putting it. To quote one teacher, "I just want to know what kind of a monster works in test prep. Like, how do you even view people?" I'll say this for that teacher's quote: it wasn't said to my face, but it was said prior to meeting me. In that teacher's defense, I sometimes wonder the same about many who work in test prep, but my misgivings are usually limited to those who are in it for a quick buck (including, amusingly enough, a large cohort of burnt-out former teachers.).

work. Because I worked as a seventh grade math teacher and spend my free time researching literacy,[161] I'm in that curious position of having the interest and ability to work with preliminary students without ever exposing them to an ACT or SAT. Mostly, these students serve as guinea pigs for whichever mad theory I intend to explore on them.

I am, of course, quite honest about this, and yet parents allow me to experiment widely and madly upon their children.[162] From my experiments, I've noted a few things, which, while many will appear obvious, may prove useful for those enterprising students[163] who wish to rule the standardized testing world instead of being ruled by it. These notes are the sort of study that can be quite helpful in building a base upon which any future self-studying or tutor-aided test prep can build.

If you're really confused about where to start, I strongly suggest that you return to the "Read" chapter. If you wish to save those works, however, you should find a wealth of material here. For improving your reading comprehension, I strongly suggest reading (not watching) *The Adventures of Sherlock Holmes*, *The Best American Science and Nature Writing*,[164] *Animal Farm*, and *How to Win Friends and Influence People*.[165]

---

[161] Well, fine, I *mostly* research argumentation theory and informal logic these days, but I have spent ample hours on literacy and numeracy and still spend some time on those areas.

[162] Which is why you're reading this book right now. There's this beautiful thing about being an expert. People trust your expertise even when you say "well, this is merely conjecture, but it's conjecture that I'm pretty sure applies." I'd note that my conjectures have generally proven themselves to be well-founded, which is why you pay for experts in the first place.

[163] Or parents with dreams of enterprising students, because I'm sure there are a few parents glancing at this chapter with great interest.

[164] I'm particularly fond of the 2010 edition because you get a biography of Elon Musk, a joyful read from Jonah Lehrer before scandal rained down upon him and *The New Yorker*, and an exploration of the stock market nosedive of 2008 and 2009 that has the same level of tedious detail an SAT or ACT social science passage might have (but it's about markets crashing!). It's hard to find a better representative mix of narrative nonfiction and "college-level" writing, whatever that phrase means. Simply, if you think electric cars are cool or want to know if the shrimp you eat should actually be eaten, then pick up this book.

[165] This last book has a dreadful title. I had to read it for a speech class, and I bought

Moving along to math, you'll probably laugh at my first suggestion, but I'd suggest you hold in your mirth. There's this fun little company called *MindWare*, and it has these awesome little torture exercises called *Math Perplexors*. The math perplexors are great because they force you to grapple with the constraints of a closed-world environment (yup, just like standardized tests live in closed-world environments) while quickening your reasoning *and* arithmetic skills. No cheating, you don't get to use calculators for these. By not using a calculator, you'll be forcing your brain to actually think about numbers instead of enjoying the mesmeric[166] powers of your calculator. *Math Perplexors* will help you on the Reading and Math sections of the SAT (in particular the "no calculator" section on the SAT) and on the Reading, Math, and Science sections of the ACT. Pretty decent bang for your buck.

Now I should warn you that this isn't a good time to be a hero. Nor is it a good time to believe the book publisher's rating system. You see, Level A of *Math Perplexors* is a nightmare of a book by itself for first-timers. I've used this book with college students who were preparing

---

a hardbound copy, tore off the jacket, and added a brown paper bag jacket of my own—just so that people wouldn't be able to see the cover of what I was reading. I might suggest you do the same. Also, you don't get to cheat and buy an updated version. The new versions won't help your reading comprehension anywhere near as much. The 1981 version is the most recent you can get. None of those dumbed-down digital age versions (updated my foot). I'll note that this book is considered a classic for good reason: most of the business books you can read today are mere footnotes or slightly revised versions of this book. Even contemporary classics like *Getting to Yes* only add 10% more value *in one specific area* than *How to Win Friends and Influence People*. If you're going to read a book, read the classic that makes the most efficient use of your time. Not only will you be reading what's probably the #1 sales book of all time, you'll be reading a book that will help you improve your reading comprehension without boring you to death. Win win.

[166] I'll be honest, for most of my students the phrase siren song might be better. Stop falling in love with your calculators. Use your brains! Actually, read the article about magical formulas that most people can't understand but calculator-aided algorithms "can" in *The Best American Science and Nature Writing 2010* and then reconsider your love for the calculator! Calculators are great, but they aren't a replacement for a brain. They are a tool for your brain. Understand the difference. I'd note that your math teachers may be confused about this. Don't get lost because of their confusion.

for the LSAT, and, when they reached the "Hey, hey, we're the monkeys" or whatever that little horror section is called, they cried uncle. I've had parents who couldn't help their 6th graders with that section because they hadn't done the warmup exercises before it. Start on Level A. I know it says for ages 8 and 9. And if you've been doing these puzzles since you were that age *and* have had your parents or teacher helping you through, then sure. But for everyone else, start on Level A. I use it with all of my high school sophomores (or younger, if I take them on as students younger). I tried Level B first with a student a few years back, and we had to move back to Level A.

Part of the reason to start on Level A is because this is a *training* tool. You're trying to build speed, not frustration. You build speed by starting on things that are easier, and then you escalate speed. Use Level A to push the speed by which you can eliminate extraneous information. There are no hero points for starting at a harder level and going more slowly. This is training for your mental math and mental reasoning speed. Speed isn't everything in life, but it is important for doing well on standardized tests. Use *Math Perplexors* to help you build your speed.

For those who have the time and desire to develop skills for outlying math and science questions, I would suggest the box set of *Logic Links* which is also sold by *MindWare*. There are typos in at least three of the one hundred fifty puzzles, but aside from those few irritations (perhaps corrected now, my set is older), the puzzles are a hands-on way of improving some of the skills the ACT in particular has tested. *Logic Links* remains a favorite of my students. Most of my junior year test prep students long for the halcyon days gone by when all I tortured them with was short stories and *Logic Links*. Oh, those good ol' days.

Next up is a little book of awesomeness from *the Art of Problem Solving*. You may recognize this company from "Performance-Enhancing Accelerators." Well, they have an excellent preliminary book called *Introduction to Counting and Probability*. If you're a freshman or sophomore, buy the book with its answer key and go to town. If you can't get every single question, that's okay. If you can get most of the questions and a decent understanding of this book's concepts (again, as little calculator as possible!), then you'll find yourself ready for some of the ACT and SAT's random questions *and* you'll have much better numerical sense. Many students screw up on standardized tests because they don't actually think about the numbers in front of them. *Introduction to Counting and Probability* will help remedy that flaw. Further, as the name of the series should indicate, it will help you to become a better problem solver. Curiously enough, that skill is precisely what you need on test day. If you have a math tutor or a friend to study with, that will certainly help, but you can absolutely study on your own with the teacher's guide. That doesn't mean you'll understand every single problem, but if you can handle most of them, then you'll find yourself ready to transform into a testing freak on game day when it arrives your junior year.

If you're quite concerned about your science knowledge, I might suggest poking around with *Filament Games'* offerings. In addition to *Citizen Science* and *Resilient Planet*, which are for high school students, *Filament Games* offers a suite of science games geared toward junior high students. Remember that I started this paragraph with the phrase "quite concerned," so don't be offended that I've suggested a learning solution that is possibly beneath your grade level. *Filament Games* provides excellent learning environments which can help shore up areas of scientific weakness. Most of the ACT Science section involves remembering some basics of scientific reasoning and then being able to apply those basics when you're exposed to weird graphs and other displays of information. If that's the case, wouldn't a game which explores those very same things be of use to you? Plus, it might not be quite so boring as some science teachers manage to make science class. I have students in AP Chemistry classes who basically take practice tests every week instead of being taught anything, and I have other students whose chemistry classes don't even provide every student with a textbook. So I recognize that your science classes might be lacking. Use

Filament Games to spice up your science exploration and enhance your science skills. There are worse ways of getting ready for the ACT (and somewhat SAT[167]).

The above should provide you with an ample amount to explore, but you may be wondering what more you can do. Such wonderment would best be answered by your teachers, coaches, guardians, or mentors. The people in your life can provide you with a wealth of interesting worlds to explore. Standardized tests are asking who has read the most broadly. Let those around you help you to grow. My general suggestion is that for every book you want to read, you should also try reading one that will challenge you. If you are someone who prefers to read in smaller doses, for every article, blog post, or short story that you wish to read, try a challenging one. Believe me, I don't necessarily wish to read every single book that I do. Many of them, though, I'm glad to have read once I'm through. I still reward myself afterwards with reading something I want to. Find your balance, but do keep reading whatever things interest you. It's totally okay to hate ACT or SAT reading. It's understandable that some assigned school reading may appear pure tedium. Don't let those experiences teach you to hate reading as a universal category. Find your niche and roll with it.

---

[167] As a reminder, the SAT has two science reading passages in its Reading Test. Those read like *National Geographic* or a boring biology textbook. You probably don't need to study more science than you've covered already in your regular courses, but if the word "gravity" makes you shiver in fear, perhaps you should try *Filament Games'* offerings.

Acknowledgements

This book would not exist without my students, all of them. My life is the better for knowing them. Many thanks are due to my students' parents, school clients, app users, and friends in the startup community. To my family and editor, thank you for humoring me in this endeavor.

"Love the art, poor as it may be, which thou hast learned, and be content with it; and pass through the rest of life like one who has entrusted to the gods with his whole soul all that he has, making thyself neither the tyrant nor the slave of any man." Marcus Aurelius

Works Cited:

Aristotle. *Nicomachean Ethics*. Trans. C.D.C. Reeve. Hackett Publishing Company, 2014.

Aurelius, Marcus, Epictetus, and Lucius Annaeus Seneca. Stoic Six Pack: *Meditations of Marcus Aurelius, The Golden Sayings, Fragments and Discourses of Epictetus, Letters from a Stoic, and The Enchiridion*. Trans. George Long, Hastings Crossley, and Richard Mott Gunmere. Enhanced Media, 2015.

da Vinci, Leonardo. *Thoughts on Art and Life*. Trans. Maurice Baring. The Merrymount Press, 1906.

de Tocqueville. *Democracy in America: The Complete and Unabridged Volumes I and II*. Trans. Henry Reeve, A Bantam Classic, 2004.

Eliot, George. *Impressions of Theophrastus Such, Essays and Leaves from a Note-Book by George Eliot*. Little, Brown, and Co., 1900.

Greever, Garland, and Easley S. Jones. *The Century Handbook of Writing*. Revised ed. The Century Co., 1918.

Hesiod. *Complete Works*. Delphi Classics, 2013.

Humphreys, Arthur L. *The Private Library: What We Do Know, What We Don't Know, What We Ought to Know About Our Books*. J.W. Bouton, 1897.

Kitson, Harry D. *How To Use Your Mind: A Psychology Of Study, Being A Manual For The Use Of Students And Teachers In The Administration Of Supervised Study*. J.B. Lippencott Company, 1916.

Klickmann, Flora. *The Lure of the Pen*: *A Book For Would-Be Authors*. G.P. Putnam's Sons, 1920.

Knerr, Kreigh. "Sifting Thoughts." *EdTech Digest*. 17 April 2013. 04 Jun 2016. <https://edtechdigest.wordpress.com/2013/04/17/sifting-thoughts/>

Jacks, L.P. *The Alchemy of Thought*. Henry Holt and Co., 1911.

Lippman, Walter. *Public Opinion*. Harcourt, Brace and Co., 1922.

More, Hannah. *The Works of Hannah More, Vol. II*. Harper & Brothers, 1835.

Newman, John Henry. "English Critical Essays." 1956. *Archive*. Ed. Edmund D. Jones. 03 June 2016. <https://archive.org/stream/englishcriticale00joneuoft/englishcriticale00joneuoft_djvu.txt>

Poincaré, Henri. *Science and Hypothesis*. Walter Scott Publishing, 1905.

Raleigh, Sir Walter. *Style*. Edward Arnold, 1897.

Repplier, Agnes. "Words." 1893. *Quotidiana*. Ed. Patrick Madden. 10 Apr 2007. 03 Jun 2016. <http://essays.quotidiana.org/repplier/words/>

Shelley, Mary. *Frankenstein*. Wordsworth Editions Ltd., 1999.

Southey, Robert. *Quotations Page*. 04 June 2016. <http://www.quotationspage.com/quote/2408.html>

Swift, Jonathan. *The Works of Jonathan Swift*. Henry G. Bohn, 1843.

The Italian Job. Dir. F. Gary Gray. Paramount Pictures, 2003.

The Official ACT Prep Guide, 2016-2017. John Wiley & Sons, 2016.

The Official SAT Study Guide. College Board, 2015.

The Real ACT Prep Guide: The Only Official Prep Guide from the Makers of the ACT. Peterson's, 2008.

The Smashing Pumpkins. "Bullet with Butterfly Wings." *Mellon Collie and the Infinite Sadness*. Virgin, 1995.

Made in the USA
Lexington, KY
19 May 2019